© 2024 by FAISAL JAMIL. All rights reserved.

Title: The Complete Guide to Fast Moving Consumer Goods (FMCG)

This book, along with its contents encompassing text, illustrations, images, diagrams, and other creative elements, is the exclusive property of FAISAL JAMIL and is safeguarded by copyright law.

FAISAL JAMIL asserts full ownership and retains all rights to this book. No part of this publication may be reproduced, distributed, or transmitted in any form or by any means, such as photocopying, recording, or electronic methods, without prior written consent from the copyright holder. Brief quotations in critical reviews and certain noncommercial uses permitted by copyright law are exceptions.

This copyright notice applies to all editions, formats, and translations of the book, whether in print, digital, or any other medium or technology existing now or developed in the future. Unauthorized use or infringement may result in legal action and pursuit of remedies under applicable copyright laws.

While efforts have been made to ensure accuracy and reliability, FAISAL JAMIL does not guarantee the completeness or suitability of the information. Readers are responsible for evaluating and using the content judiciously.

FAISAL JAMIL reserves the right to make changes, updates, or corrections to the book without prior notice. Inclusion of third-party materials or references does not imply endorsement or affiliation unless used under fair use principles or with proper permissions and attributions.

For permissions, inquiries, or requests regarding the book's use, please contact FAISAL JAMIL through official channels listed on their Amazon author page or provided email address.

This comprehensive copyright notice serves to protect FAISAL JAMIL'S intellectual property rights, maintain content control, and inform users about associated restrictions and permissions.

Warm regards,

FAISAL JAMIL

For your feedback and reviews:

https://www.amazon.com/author/faisal-jamil

Email: faisaljamilauthor@gmail.com

About the author

Certainly! Faisal Jamil is a multifaceted individual with a diverse set of skills and experiences. With a strong foundation in computer knowledge since childhood, he has developed a deep understanding of technology that informs his work as a content writer. Faisal also possesses digital skills, which further enhance his abilities in various digital platforms and technologies.

Beyond his professional endeavors, Faisal Jamil has also excelled in the martial arts, particularly Shotokan Karate, where he achieved the prestigious rank of first Dan black belt. This achievement speaks to his dedication, discipline, and commitment to personal growth and mastery.

In his professional life, Faisal Jamil has carved out a successful career in sales management within the Fast Moving Consumer Goods (FMCG) sector. His roles in various FMCG companies have honed his skills in strategic planning, team leadership, and business development. Faisal's ability to drive sales and achieve targets has been instrumental in his career progression, showcasing his talent for identifying opportunities and delivering results.

Faisal is also deeply interested in business investment strategies, planning, and execution. His understanding of these areas has been key to his success in the business world, allowing him to make informed decisions and implement effective strategies. His ability to navigate the complexities of investment planning and execution has set him apart as a strategic thinker and a valuable asset in any business endeavor.

Overall, Faisal Jamil is a dynamic individual who combines his passion for technology, martial arts, sales management, digital skills, and business investment strategies to achieve success in diverse fields. His journey is a testament to his versatility, resilience, and continuous pursuit of excellence.

Yours Sincerely

FAISAL JAMIL

For your feedback and reviews:

https://www.amazon.com/author/faisal-jamil

Email: faisaljamilauthor@gmail.com

THE COMPLETE GUIDE TO FAST MOVING CONSUMER GOODS (FMCG)

Table of Content

Preface

Chapter 1: Introduction to FMCG

Chapter 2: Evolution of the FMCG Industry

Chapter 3: Global FMCG Market Overview

Chapter 4: Consumer Behavior in FMCG

Chapter 5: Marketing Strategies in FMCG

Chapter 6: Brand Management in FMCG

Chapter 7: Supply Chain Management in FMCG

Chapter 8: Retailing and Channel Management

Chapter 9: Packaging and Labeling in FMCG

Chapter 10: Technology in FMCG

Chapter 11: Quality Control and Regulatory Compliance

Chapter 12: Trends in FMCG Innovation

Chapter 13: Sustainability Practices in FMCG

Chapter 14: Challenges Facing the FMCG Industry

Chapter 15: Future Outlook for the FMCG Industry

Chapter 16: Digital Transformation in FMCG

Chapter 17: Cross-border Expansion Strategies

Chapter 18: Brand Loyalty Programs

Chapter 19: Crisis Management in FMCG

Chapter 20: Private Label Brands

Chapter 21: Direct-to-Consumer (DTC) Trends

Chapter 22: Mergers and Acquisitions in FMCG

Chapter 23: Social Media Marketing in FMCG

Chapter 24: Health and Wellness Trends

Chapter 25: Packaging Innovations

Chapter 26: Retailer Relationships

Chapter 27: Crisis Communication

Chapter 28: Pricing Strategies

Chapter 29: Product Life Cycle Management

Chapter 30: E-commerce Strategies

Chapter 31: Rural Marketing

Chapter 32: Corporate Social Responsibility (CSR) in FMCG

Chapter 33: Trade Promotion Management

Chapter 34: Product Differentiation

Chapter 35: Outsourcing and Contract Manufacturing

Chapter 36: Omni-channel Retailing

Chapter 37: Emerging Technologies in FMCG

Chapter 38: Inclusive Marketing

Chapter 39: Employee Training and Development

Chapter 40: Influencer Marketing

Chapter 41: Risk Management

Chapter 42: Product Innovation Process

Chapter 43: Customer Relationship Management (CRM)

Chapter 44: Global Sourcing and Procurement

Chapter 45: Green Marketing

Chapter 46: Product Placement and Merchandising

Chapter 47: Data Privacy and Security

Chapter 48: Legal and Regulatory Compliance

Chapter 49: Market Research and Consumer Insights

Chapter 50: Conclusion and Future Outlook

Preface

Welcome to "The Complete Guide to Fast Moving Consumer Goods (FMCG)"! This book is designed to be a comprehensive and practical resource for anyone looking to understand the dynamic world of FMCG. Whether you are a seasoned industry professional, a student studying business or marketing, or simply curious about how FMCG products make their way to your shelves, this book is for you.

The FMCG industry is fast-paced, competitive, and constantly evolving. Products that fall into this category, such as food and beverages, personal care items, household goods, and other consumables, are essential parts of our daily lives. Understanding the complexities of this industry—from production and distribution to marketing and sales—is crucial for anyone looking to succeed in this space.

In this book, we will explore a wide range of topics related to FMCG, including the definition and characteristics of FMCG products, the history and evolution of the industry, global market trends, consumer behavior, marketing strategies, supply chain management, retailing, packaging, technology, quality control, regulatory compliance, and sustainability practices.

Each chapter is designed to provide you with valuable insights, practical tips, and real-world examples that you can apply to your own work or studies. Whether you are interested in learning about the latest trends in product development, exploring innovative marketing strategies, or understanding the impact of technology on the industry, this book has something for you.

I hope that you find this book informative, engaging, and inspiring. The FMCG industry is a vibrant and exciting field, and I am thrilled to be able to share my knowledge and passion for this industry with you. So, sit back, relax, and enjoy "The Complete Guide to Fast Moving Consumer Goods (FMCG)"!

Chapter 1: Introduction to FMCG

A: Definition and Characteristics of FMCG Products

Fast Moving Consumer Goods (FMCG) are products that are sold quickly and at a relatively low cost. These goods are also referred to as consumer packaged goods (CPG) and include items such as food and beverages, personal care products, cleaning supplies, and over-the-counter drugs. The key characteristics of FMCG products are:

1: Perishability: Many FMCG products have a limited shelf life and need to be consumed or used within a short period. Examples include fresh food items, dairy products, and certain cosmetics.

2: Frequent Purchase: FMCG products are items that consumers purchase frequently, often as part of their routine shopping trips. These products are essential for daily living and include items like toothpaste, shampoo, and bread.

3: Low Cost: FMCG products are typically priced low to moderate, making them affordable for a wide range of consumers. This pricing strategy helps drive volume sales.

4: Rapid Consumption: FMCG products are designed for rapid consumption or use. This means that consumers go through these products quickly and need to replenish them regularly.

5: Brand Loyalty: Many FMCG products benefit from strong brand loyalty, with consumers often sticking to their preferred brands for these everyday items.

6: Mass Marketing: FMCG products are often mass-marketed through various channels such as television, print, and digital media to reach a large audience.

B: Importance of FMCG in the Global Economy

The FMCG sector plays a significant role in the global economy for several reasons:

1: Employment: The FMCG sector is a major employer worldwide, providing jobs in manufacturing, distribution, retail, and marketing. It is a source of livelihood for millions of people, particularly in developing countries.

2: Revenue Generation: FMCG companies generate substantial revenue, contributing to the overall economic growth of countries. These companies pay taxes, invest in infrastructure, and support local communities.

3: Consumer Spending: FMCG products are essential items that consumers purchase regularly, regardless of economic conditions. This consistent demand helps stabilize the economy during downturns.

4: Innovation and Technology: The FMCG sector is a hub of innovation, constantly developing new products, packaging, and marketing strategies. This innovation drives technological advancements and benefits other industries.

5: Global Trade: FMCG products are traded globally, contributing to international trade and economic interdependence. This trade stimulates economic growth and creates opportunities for businesses to expand globally.

6: Consumer Welfare: FMCG products improve the quality of life for consumers by providing essential goods that meet their daily needs. These products enhance health, hygiene, and overall well-being.

In conclusion, FMCG products are an integral part of the global economy, driving growth, employment, and innovation. Their affordability, frequent purchase, and widespread availability make them indispensable for consumers around the world.

Chapter 2: Evolution of the FMCG Industry

A: Historical Overview of FMCG

The FMCG industry has a rich history that dates back to ancient times. The concept of trading essential goods for everyday use has been a part of human civilization for centuries. However, the modern FMCG industry began to take shape during the Industrial Revolution in the 18th and 19th centuries.

During this period, advancements in manufacturing, transportation, and communication revolutionized the way goods were produced and distributed. Mass production techniques allowed for the efficient manufacture of consumer goods, making them more affordable and accessible to a wider population.

One of the earliest examples of FMCG products is soap, which became popular in the 19th century due to improved hygiene practices. Other early FMCG products include tea, coffee, and canned goods, which were introduced to meet the growing demands of urban populations.

The 20th century saw further advancements in the FMCG industry, with the introduction of new products and packaging innovations. The rise of supermarkets and mass marketing techniques also contributed to the growth of the industry, making FMCG products more readily available to consumers.

In recent decades, the FMCG industry has continued to evolve, driven by changing consumer preferences, technological advancements, and globalization. E-commerce has emerged as a major distribution channel, allowing consumers to purchase FMCG products online and have them delivered to their doorstep.

Overall, the FMCG industry has undergone significant transformations over the years, adapting to changing market conditions and consumer demands to become one of the largest and most dynamic sectors in the global economy.

B: Key Milestones and Developments

1: Mass Production: The introduction of mass production techniques in the 19th century revolutionized the FMCG industry, allowing for the efficient manufacture of goods on a large scale.

2: Branding and Advertising: The late 19th and early 20th centuries saw the rise of branding and advertising, with companies using these techniques to differentiate their products and attract consumers.

3: Packaging Innovations: The development of new packaging materials and designs in the 20th century improved the shelf life and appeal of FMCG products, leading to increased sales.

4: Retail Revolution: The introduction of supermarkets and hypermarkets in the mid-20th century changed the way FMCG products were sold, offering consumers a wide range of choices under one roof.

5: Globalization: The latter half of the 20th century saw the globalization of the FMCG industry, with companies expanding into new markets and adapting their products to suit local tastes and preferences.

6: E-commerce: The rise of the internet and e-commerce in the 21st century has transformed the way FMCG products are bought and sold, providing consumers with greater convenience and choice.

7: Sustainability: In recent years, there has been a growing emphasis on sustainability in the FMCG industry, with companies focusing on reducing their environmental impact and promoting eco-friendly products.

These milestones and developments have shaped the evolution of the FMCG industry, making it one of the most dynamic and innovative sectors in the global economy.

Chapter 3: Global FMCG Market Overview

A: Market Size and Growth Trends

The global Fast Moving Consumer Goods (FMCG) market is vast and dynamic, characterized by rapid changes in consumer preferences, competitive pressures, and technological advancements. The market encompasses a wide range of products, including food and beverages, personal care products, household goods, and more.

According to market research reports, the global FMCG market was valued at over $5 trillion in 2020 and is projected to continue growing at a steady pace in the coming years. The growth of the FMCG market is driven by several factors, including:

1: Population Growth: The world's population is increasing, particularly in emerging markets, leading to higher demand for FMCG products.

2: Urbanization: The ongoing trend of urbanization is driving changes in lifestyle and consumption patterns, leading to increased demand for convenience and packaged goods.

3: Rising Disposable Income: As incomes rise, consumers are able to spend more on discretionary items, including FMCG products.

4: Changing Consumer Preferences: Consumers are increasingly seeking products that offer health benefits, convenience, and sustainability, driving innovation and new product development in the FMCG sector.

5: E-commerce Growth: The growth of e-commerce has opened up new distribution channels for FMCG products, allowing companies to reach a wider audience and drive sales.

B: Regional Dynamics and Key Markets

The FMCG market is not homogeneous and varies significantly across regions and countries. Some regions, such as Asia-Pacific and Latin America, are experiencing rapid growth due to rising populations, urbanization, and increasing disposable incomes. These regions are seen as key growth markets for FMCG companies looking to expand their presence.

In Asia-Pacific, countries like China and India are major contributors to the growth of the FMCG market. These countries have large populations and a rising middle class, creating a significant demand for FMCG products. Other key markets in the region include Japan, South Korea, and Indonesia.

In Europe, the FMCG market is more mature but still offers opportunities for growth, particularly in Eastern Europe. Countries like Russia and Poland are experiencing economic growth and rising consumer spending, making them attractive markets for FMCG companies.

In North America, the FMCG market is characterized by high levels of competition and consumer sophistication. The United States is the largest market in the region, with a strong demand for premium and organic products.

In Latin America, countries like Brazil and Mexico are driving growth in the FMCG market. These countries have large populations and a growing middle class, creating opportunities for FMCG companies to expand their presence.

Overall, the global FMCG market is dynamic and diverse, offering opportunities for growth and innovation for companies willing to adapt to changing consumer trends and market dynamics.

Chapter 4: Consumer Behavior in FMCG

A: Factors Influencing Consumer Purchasing Decisions

Consumer purchasing decisions in the FMCG sector are influenced by a variety of factors, including:

1: Price: Price is often a key factor for consumers when choosing FMCG products. Consumers are more likely to purchase products that offer value for money and fit within their budget.

2: Quality: Quality is another important consideration for consumers. They are more likely to choose products that are perceived to be of high quality and reliable.

3: Brand Reputation: Brand reputation plays a significant role in consumer purchasing decisions. Consumers are often loyal to well-established brands that they trust.

4: Product Features: The features and benefits of a product can influence consumer choices. Products that offer unique features or benefits are more likely to attract consumers.

5: Packaging: Packaging can also influence consumer purchasing decisions. Eye-catching and informative packaging can make a product stand out on the shelf.

6: Convenience: Convenience is an important factor for many consumers. Products that are easy to use or consume are more likely to be chosen.

7: Health and Wellness: With growing health consciousness, consumers are increasingly choosing FMCG products that are perceived to be healthy and nutritious.

8: Social Influences: Social factors, such as recommendations from friends and family, as well as social media influencers, can also influence consumer purchasing decisions.

B: Brand Loyalty and Switching Behavior

Brand loyalty is a key factor in the FMCG sector, with many consumers sticking to their preferred brands for years.

Brand loyalty is often built through consistent quality, effective marketing, and positive consumer experiences.

However, consumers' loyalty to brands is not absolute, and they may switch to other brands for various reasons, including:

1: Price: Consumers may switch to a different brand if they find a similar product at a lower price.

2: Quality Issues: Quality-related problems, such as product defects or changes in product formulation, can lead to consumers switching brands.

3: Availability: If a preferred brand is not readily available, consumers may choose a different brand.

4: Changing Preferences: Consumer preferences and tastes may change over time, leading to a switch in brands.

5: Promotions and Discounts: Promotional offers and discounts can influence consumers to switch brands temporarily.

Understanding consumer behavior and the factors that influence purchasing decisions is crucial for FMCG companies to develop effective marketing strategies and build strong, lasting relationships with their customers.

Chapter 5: Marketing Strategies in FMCG

A: Product Development and Innovation

Product development and innovation are crucial for FMCG companies to stay competitive and meet changing consumer demands. Some key strategies in this area include:

1: New Product Development: FMCG companies continuously develop new products to cater to evolving consumer preferences. This involves market research, product design, and testing.

2: Line Extensions: Extending existing product lines with new flavors, variants, or packaging sizes can help companies attract new customers and increase sales from existing ones.

3: Product Improvements: Regularly updating and improving existing products based on consumer feedback and market trends can help companies maintain customer loyalty.

4: Innovation: Introducing innovative products that offer unique benefits or address specific consumer needs can help companies differentiate themselves in the market.

B: Pricing Strategies

Pricing strategies in the FMCG sector are influenced by factors such as competition, cost of production, and consumer perception. Some common pricing strategies include:

1: Penetration Pricing: Setting a low initial price to attract customers and gain market share quickly.

2: Skimming Pricing: Setting a high initial price to maximize profits from customers willing to pay a premium for new products.

3: Competitive Pricing: Setting prices based on competitors' prices to remain competitive in the market.

4: Value-Based Pricing: Setting prices based on the perceived value of the product to the customer.

C: Distribution Channels

Distribution channels play a crucial role in the success of FMCG products, ensuring they reach consumers efficiently. Common distribution channels in the FMCG sector include:

1: Retail Stores: FMCG products are often sold through supermarkets, convenience stores, and other retail outlets.

2: Online Retail: The growth of e-commerce has led to an increase in online sales of FMCG products.

3: Direct Sales: Some FMCG companies use direct sales channels, such as door-to-door sales or company-owned retail outlets.

4: Wholesalers and Distributors: FMCG companies often work with wholesalers and distributors to reach retailers and ultimately consumers.

D: Promotional Tactics

Promotional tactics are used by FMCG companies to create awareness, generate interest, and drive sales of their products. Some common promotional tactics include:

1: Advertising: Advertising through various channels such as television, radio, print, and digital media to reach a wide audience.

2: Sales Promotions: Offering discounts, coupons, and special offers to incentivize purchase.

3: Sponsorship and Events: Sponsoring events or sports teams to increase brand visibility and association.

4: Product Sampling: Offering free samples of products to encourage trial and purchase.

5: Social Media Marketing: Using social media platforms to engage with consumers and promote products.

Effective marketing strategies in the FMCG sector require a deep understanding of consumer behavior, market dynamics, and competitive landscape. By leveraging product development, pricing, distribution, and promotional strategies, FMCG companies can effectively reach and engage with their target audience, driving sales and building brand loyalty.

Chapter 6: Brand Management in FMCG

A: Building and Managing Strong Brands

Building and managing strong brands is essential for FMCG companies to differentiate themselves in a competitive market and build customer loyalty. Some key strategies for brand management include:

1: Brand Identity: Developing a strong brand identity that reflects the company's values, personality, and unique selling proposition (USP).

2: Brand Positioning: Positioning the brand in the minds of consumers to differentiate it from competitors and create a unique value proposition.

3: Brand Image: Managing the brand's image through consistent messaging, visual identity, and customer interactions to build trust and credibility.

4: Brand Communication: Communicating the brand's message effectively through various channels, such as advertising, packaging, and digital media.

5: Brand Equity: Building brand equity by creating positive associations with the brand and ensuring customer loyalty and advocacy.

6: Brand Consistency: Maintaining consistency in branding elements, such as logo, colors, and messaging, across all touchpoints to reinforce brand identity.

B: Brand Extensions and Brand Loyalty Programs

Brand extensions and loyalty programs are strategies used by FMCG companies to leverage their existing brand equity and build customer loyalty.

1: Brand Extensions: Introducing new products or product variants under an existing brand name to capitalize on its reputation and customer loyalty.

2: Co-Branding: Partnering with other brands to create co-branded products or promotions that leverage each brand's strengths and appeal to a wider audience.

3: Loyalty Programs: Implementing loyalty programs, such as reward points or discounts for repeat purchases, to incentivize customers to remain loyal to the brand.

4: Customer Relationship Management (CRM): Using CRM systems to track customer interactions and tailor marketing efforts to individual customer preferences, increasing brand loyalty.

5: Brand Advocacy: Encouraging satisfied customers to become brand advocates by sharing their positive experiences with others, thereby increasing brand loyalty and awareness.

Effective brand management in the FMCG sector requires a deep understanding of consumer behavior, market trends, and competitive dynamics. By building and managing strong brands, FMCG companies can create a sustainable competitive advantage and drive long-term success.

Chapter 7: Supply Chain Management in FMCG

A: Importance of Efficient Supply Chain Management

Efficient supply chain management is crucial for FMCG companies to ensure the timely delivery of products to customers, minimize costs, and maintain high levels of customer satisfaction. Some key reasons why supply chain management is important in the FMCG sector include:

1: Meeting Customer Demand: FMCG products have a short shelf life and high demand variability. Efficient supply chain management ensures that products are available when and where customers need them.

2: Cost Reduction: A well-managed supply chain can help FMCG companies reduce costs associated with production, transportation, and inventory holding.

3: Improved Customer Service: A responsive and reliable supply chain helps FMCG companies deliver products to customers quickly and accurately, enhancing customer satisfaction and loyalty.

4: Competitive Advantage: An efficient supply chain can be a source of competitive advantage, allowing FMCG companies to respond quickly to market changes and customer demands.

B: Logistics and Distribution

Logistics and distribution play a critical role in the FMCG supply chain, ensuring that products are delivered to customers efficiently and cost-effectively. Some key aspects of logistics and distribution in the FMCG sector include:

1: Transportation: Selecting the most appropriate modes of transportation (road, rail, air, sea) based on factors such as cost, speed, and reliability.

2: Warehousing: Managing warehouses and distribution centers to ensure efficient storage, handling, and dispatch of products.

3: Order Fulfillment: Processing customer orders quickly and accurately to ensure timely delivery.

4: Reverse Logistics: Managing product returns and exchanges efficiently to minimize costs and customer dissatisfaction.

5: Distribution Network Design: Designing an optimal distribution network to ensure products reach customers in the most efficient manner.

C: Inventory Management

Effective inventory management is essential for FMCG companies to balance the costs of holding inventory with the need to meet customer demand. Some key aspects of inventory management in the FMCG sector include:

1: Demand Forecasting: Forecasting demand for FMCG products accurately to ensure the right level of inventory is maintained.

2: Just-in-Time (JIT) Inventory: Using JIT principles to minimize inventory holding costs while ensuring products are available when needed.

3: Inventory Optimization: Using inventory optimization techniques to determine the optimal levels of inventory to hold based on factors such as demand variability and lead times.

4: Stock Keeping Units (SKUs) Management: Managing the number and variety of SKUs to ensure efficient inventory management.

5: Inventory Tracking: Implementing systems to track inventory levels in real-time and minimize the risk of stockouts or overstocking.

In conclusion, supply chain management is a critical function in the FMCG sector, ensuring that products are delivered to customers efficiently, cost-effectively, and on time. Effective management of logistics, distribution, and inventory is essential for FMCG companies to maintain high levels of customer satisfaction and competitive advantage.

Chapter 8: Retailing and Channel Management

A: Retail Landscape in FMCG

The retail landscape in the FMCG sector is diverse and dynamic, with various types of retailers playing a role in the distribution and sale of FMCG products. Some key aspects of the retail landscape in FMCG include:

1: Supermarkets and Hypermarkets: These large-format stores offer a wide range of FMCG products, including groceries, personal care items, and household goods. They often provide a one-stop shopping experience for consumers.

2: Convenience Stores: Convenience stores are small retail outlets that offer a limited selection of FMCG products, primarily focusing on items that consumers need quickly or on the go.

3: Online Retail: The growth of e-commerce has led to the emergence of online retailers selling FMCG products. These retailers offer convenience and a wide selection of products, appealing to a growing number of consumers.

4: Specialty Stores: Specialty stores focus on specific categories of FMCG products, such as health foods, organic products, or gourmet foods. These stores cater to consumers looking for unique or high-quality products.

5: Discount Retailers: Discount retailers offer FMCG products at discounted prices, appealing to price-conscious consumers. These retailers often sell products in bulk or at lower margins than traditional retailers.

B: Channel Strategies and Partnerships

Channel strategies and partnerships play a crucial role in the distribution of FMCG products, helping companies reach their target markets efficiently and effectively. Some key channel strategies and partnerships in the FMCG sector include:

1: Retailer Partnerships: FMCG companies often form partnerships with retailers to ensure their products are available in stores. These partnerships may involve exclusive distribution agreements or joint marketing efforts.

2: Direct-to-Consumer (DTC) Channels: Some FMCG companies sell their products directly to consumers through their own online stores or physical outlets. This allows companies to bypass traditional retail channels and maintain control over the customer experience.

3: Distributor Networks: FMCG companies may work with distributors to reach retailers in different regions or countries. Distributors help companies manage logistics and expand their reach in the market.

4: Online Retail Partnerships: FMCG companies may partner with online retailers to sell their products through e-commerce platforms. These partnerships help companies reach a wider audience and tap into the growing online shopping trend.

5: Co-Marketing Partnerships: FMCG companies may collaborate with other brands or retailers on co-marketing campaigns or promotions. These partnerships can help companies reach new customers and increase brand visibility.

In conclusion, retailing and channel management are critical aspects of the FMCG sector, helping companies reach their target markets and drive sales. By understanding the retail landscape and developing effective channel strategies and partnerships, FMCG companies can maximize their distribution reach and achieve their business objectives.

Chapter 9: Packaging and Labeling in FMCG

A: Importance of Packaging in FMCG

Packaging plays a crucial role in the FMCG sector, serving multiple purposes beyond just containing and protecting the product. Some key importance of packaging in FMCG include:

1: Protection: Packaging protects FMCG products from damage, spoilage, and contamination during storage, transportation, and handling.

2: Preservation: Packaging helps preserve the quality, freshness, and shelf life of FMCG products, ensuring they remain safe and usable for consumers.

3: Information: Packaging provides important information to consumers, such as product ingredients, nutritional information, usage instructions, and expiry dates.

4: Branding: Packaging serves as a key branding tool, helping FMCG companies differentiate their products from competitors and create a strong brand identity.

5: Marketing: Packaging is an important marketing tool, as it can attract consumers' attention, communicate product benefits, and influence purchasing decisions.

6: Convenience: Packaging can enhance the convenience of FMCG products for consumers, such as easy-to-open packaging, portion-controlled packaging, and resealable packaging.

B: Sustainable Packaging Trends

Sustainable packaging is a growing trend in the FMCG sector, driven by increasing consumer awareness of environmental issues and regulatory pressures to reduce waste. Some key sustainable packaging trends in FMCG include:

1: Use of Recyclable Materials: FMCG companies are increasingly using recyclable materials, such as paper, cardboard, glass, and certain plastics, to reduce the environmental impact of packaging.

2: Biodegradable and Compostable Packaging: FMCG companies are exploring biodegradable and compostable packaging materials, which break down naturally in the environment and reduce landfill waste.

3: Lightweight Packaging: FMCG companies are designing packaging that is lightweight yet strong, reducing the amount of material used and lowering transportation costs and emissions.

4: Minimalist Packaging: FMCG companies are simplifying packaging designs to reduce excess packaging material and improve recyclability.

5: Reusable Packaging: FMCG companies are exploring reusable packaging options, such as refillable containers and packaging loops, to reduce single-use packaging waste.

6: Smart Packaging: FMCG companies are incorporating smart packaging technologies, such as QR codes and RFID tags, to provide consumers with information about product origins, ingredients, and recycling instructions.

Sustainable packaging is not only environmentally friendly but also aligns with consumer preferences for eco-friendly products. FMCG companies that embrace sustainable packaging can enhance their brand image, reduce costs, and contribute to a more sustainable future.

Chapter 10: Technology in FMCG

A: Role of Technology in Product Development and Marketing

Technology plays a crucial role in product development and marketing in the FMCG sector, enabling companies to innovate, streamline processes, and reach customers more effectively. Some key roles of technology in FMCG include:

1: Product Development: Technology is used in product development to create new formulations, flavors, and packaging designs. Tools such as computer-aided design (CAD) and simulation software help companies test and refine product concepts before production.

2: Market Research: Technology enables FMCG companies to conduct market research more efficiently, gathering data on consumer preferences, trends, and competitor activities. Tools such as online surveys, social media analytics, and big data analysis help companies gain insights into consumer behavior and market dynamics.

3: Manufacturing: Technology is used in manufacturing to improve efficiency, quality, and flexibility. Automated production lines, robotics, and advanced manufacturing techniques help FMCG companies produce goods faster and with fewer errors.

4: Supply Chain Management: Technology is used in supply chain management to track inventory, manage logistics, and optimize distribution networks. Systems such as enterprise resource planning (ERP) and warehouse management systems (WMS) help companies streamline operations and reduce costs.

5: Marketing and Advertising: Technology is used in marketing and advertising to reach consumers through digital channels. Tools such as social media, search engine optimization (SEO), and online advertising platforms help FMCG companies target and engage with consumers more effectively.

B: Impact of E-commerce and Digital Platforms

E-commerce and digital platforms have had a profound impact on the FMCG sector, transforming the way products are bought and sold. Some key impacts of e-commerce and digital platforms in FMCG include:

1: Increased Reach: E-commerce has enabled FMCG companies to reach consumers in geographically diverse locations, expanding their market reach and customer base.

2: Direct-to-Consumer (DTC) Sales: E-commerce allows FMCG companies to sell directly to consumers through their own online stores, bypassing traditional retail channels and improving profit margins.

3: Enhanced Customer Experience: Digital platforms provide FMCG companies with opportunities to engage with customers in new ways, such as through personalized offers, loyalty programs, and interactive content.

4: Data Analytics: E-commerce and digital platforms generate vast amounts of data that can be analyzed to gain insights into consumer behavior and preferences. This data can be used to tailor marketing campaigns, improve product offerings, and enhance customer service.

5: Competitive Landscape: E-commerce has increased competition in the FMCG sector, as companies compete for online visibility and market share. This has led to increased innovation and investment in digital technologies.

Overall, technology, including e-commerce and digital platforms, is reshaping the FMCG sector, driving innovation, improving efficiency, and enhancing the customer experience. FMCG companies that embrace technology and adapt to changing consumer preferences and market dynamics are likely to succeed in this rapidly evolving landscape.

Chapter 11: Quality Control and Regulatory Compliance

A: Quality Standards in FMCG

Quality control is a critical aspect of FMCG production, ensuring that products meet the required standards of safety, efficacy, and quality. Some key quality standards in the FMCG sector include:

1: ISO Standards: The International Organization for Standardization (ISO) has developed a series of standards, such as ISO 9001 for quality management systems and ISO 22000 for food safety management, which are widely used in the FMCG industry.

2: Good Manufacturing Practices (GMP): GMP guidelines provide a framework for ensuring that products are consistently produced and controlled according to quality standards. GMP covers all aspects of production, from raw materials to finished products.

3: Hazard Analysis and Critical Control Points (HACCP): HACCP is a systematic approach to identifying, evaluating, and controlling food safety hazards. It is widely used in the food industry, including the FMCG sector, to ensure the safety of food products.

4: Product Testing and Certification: FMCG products are often subjected to testing and certification by independent laboratories to ensure they meet regulatory requirements and quality standards.

5: Quality Assurance Processes: FMCG companies implement quality assurance processes, such as regular inspections, audits, and reviews, to ensure that products meet the required standards.

B: Regulatory Challenges and Compliance Requirements

The FMCG sector is subject to a wide range of regulatory challenges and compliance requirements, which vary depending on the product category and geographical location. Some key regulatory challenges and compliance requirements in the FMCG sector include:

1: Food Safety Regulations: FMCG companies producing food and beverage products must comply with food safety regulations, which may include requirements for hygiene, sanitation, labeling, and packaging.

2: Product Labeling and Packaging Regulations: FMCG products must comply with labeling and packaging regulations, which may include requirements for ingredient lists, nutritional information, expiry dates, and recycling symbols.

3: Advertising and Marketing Regulations: FMCG companies must comply with advertising and marketing regulations, which may include restrictions on claims, endorsements, and targeted advertising to children.

4: Environmental Regulations: FMCG companies must comply with environmental regulations, which may include requirements for sustainable packaging, waste management, and emissions control.

5: Import and Export Regulations: FMCG companies involved in international trade must comply with import and export regulations, which may include requirements for customs documentation, product certification, and tariffs.

Meeting these regulatory challenges and compliance requirements is essential for FMCG companies to ensure the safety, quality, and legality of their products, and to maintain the trust and confidence of consumers and regulatory authorities alike.

Chapter 12: Trends in FMCG Innovation

A: Emerging Trends in Product Development and Packaging

1: Health and Wellness: There is a growing trend towards healthier and more natural products in the FMCG sector. Companies are developing products that are free from artificial ingredients, preservatives, and additives, and are using natural ingredients that offer health benefits.

2: Sustainability: Sustainable packaging is a major trend in FMCG innovation, with companies focusing on reducing waste, using eco-friendly materials, and adopting recyclable or biodegradable packaging solutions.

3: Convenience: Convenience is a key driver of innovation in the FMCG sector, with companies developing products that offer greater convenience to consumers, such as single-serve packaging, ready-to-eat meals, and on-the-go snacks.

4: Personalization: Personalized products are gaining popularity in the FMCG sector, with companies offering customized products to meet the specific needs and preferences of individual consumers.

5: Digitalization: Digital technologies are being integrated into FMCG products and packaging, enabling features such as smart packaging, interactive labels, and online ordering through QR codes or NFC tags.

B: Case Studies of Successful Innovations

1: Coca-Cola Freestyle: Coca-Cola Freestyle is a touch-screen soda fountain that allows customers to choose from over 100 different drink options. The innovative technology has been successful in attracting customers and increasing sales for Coca-Cola.

2: Nestlé Nespresso: Nespresso is a premium coffee brand that offers a range of coffee machines and capsules for home use. The brand has been successful in creating a premium coffee experience for consumers and building a loyal customer base.

3: Amazon Dash Button: The Amazon Dash Button is a small, Wi-Fi-enabled device that allows customers to reorder commonly used household products with the press of a button. The innovative device has simplified the shopping experience for customers and increased sales for Amazon and its partners.

4: Procter & Gamble Tide Pods: Tide Pods are single-use laundry detergent pods that contain a pre-measured amount of detergent. The innovative packaging has been successful in providing convenience to consumers and reducing waste.

5: Beyond Meat: Beyond Meat is a plant-based meat substitute that has gained popularity among consumers looking for healthier and more sustainable food options. The innovative product has been successful in tapping into the growing trend towards plant-based diets.

These case studies highlight the importance of innovation in the FMCG sector and demonstrate how companies that embrace innovation can gain a competitive edge and meet the evolving needs of consumers.

Chapter 13: Sustainability Practices in FMCG

A: Environmental Impact of FMCG Products

The FMCG sector has a significant environmental impact, primarily due to the production, packaging, and distribution of products. Some key environmental impacts of FMCG products include:

1: Resource Depletion: The production of FMCG products often requires large amounts of natural resources, such as water, energy, and raw materials, leading to resource depletion and environmental degradation.

2: Greenhouse Gas Emissions: The manufacturing, transportation, and disposal of FMCG products contribute to greenhouse gas emissions, which contribute to climate change and global warming.

3: Waste Generation: FMCG products contribute to the generation of waste, including packaging waste and product waste, which can pollute the environment and harm wildlife.

4: Water Pollution: The production and use of FMCG products can lead to water pollution, as chemicals and pollutants from manufacturing processes and product use can enter water bodies and harm aquatic ecosystems.

B: Sustainable Sourcing and Production Practices

To address these environmental impacts, FMCG companies are increasingly adopting sustainable sourcing and production practices. Some key sustainable sourcing and production practices in the FMCG sector include:

1: Sustainable Agriculture: FMCG companies are sourcing raw materials from sustainable agriculture practices, such as organic farming, agroforestry, and regenerative agriculture, which help protect biodiversity, reduce chemical use, and improve soil health.

2: Renewable Energy: FMCG companies are transitioning to renewable energy sources, such as solar, wind, and hydroelectric power, to reduce greenhouse gas emissions and reliance on fossil fuels.

3: Water Conservation: FMCG companies are implementing water conservation measures, such as recycling and reusing water in production processes, and investing in water-efficient technologies to reduce water consumption.

4: Waste Reduction: FMCG companies are working to reduce waste generation through initiatives such as lightweight packaging, recyclable materials, and product redesigns to minimize packaging waste.

5: Supply Chain Transparency: FMCG companies are increasing transparency in their supply chains to ensure that raw materials are sourced ethically and sustainably, and to address issues such as deforestation, habitat destruction, and human rights abuses.

By adopting these sustainable sourcing and production practices, FMCG companies can reduce their environmental impact, improve their reputation with consumers and stakeholders, and contribute to a more sustainable future.

Chapter 14: Challenges Facing the FMCG Industry

A: Competitive Landscape and Market Saturation

1: Intense Competition: The FMCG industry is highly competitive, with numerous players vying for market share. Companies must constantly innovate and differentiate their products to stand out in a crowded market.

2: Market Saturation: Many FMCG markets are saturated, with little room for growth. This makes it challenging for companies to expand their customer base and increase sales.

3: Changing Consumer Preferences: Consumer preferences in the FMCG sector can change rapidly, making it difficult for companies to anticipate and respond to shifting trends.

4: Private Label Brands: Private label brands, or store brands, are gaining popularity among consumers, posing a threat to traditional FMCG brands.

5: E-commerce Disruption: The rise of e-commerce has disrupted the traditional retail model, forcing FMCG companies to adapt to new ways of selling and distributing their products.

B: Price Wars and Margin Pressures

1: Price Competition: Price competition is intense in the FMCG sector, with companies often engaging in price wars to gain market share. This puts pressure on profit margins and makes it challenging for companies to maintain profitability.

2: Retailer Bargaining Power: Retailers often have significant bargaining power over FMCG companies, exerting pressure to lower prices and reduce margins.

3: Rising Costs: FMCG companies face rising costs for raw materials, labor, and transportation, further squeezing profit margins.

4: Promotional Spending: FMCG companies often spend heavily on promotions and advertising to attract customers, further reducing margins.

5: Discounting: FMCG companies may resort to frequent discounting to stimulate sales, which can erode margins over time.

To address these challenges, FMCG companies must focus on innovation, cost efficiency, and strategic pricing strategies. By understanding the competitive landscape, anticipating changing consumer preferences, and adapting to the evolving retail environment, FMCG companies can overcome these challenges and thrive in the market.

Chapter 15: Future Outlook for the FMCG Industry

A: Emerging Markets and Growth Opportunities

1: Emerging Markets: The FMCG industry is expected to see significant growth in emerging markets, particularly in Asia, Africa, and Latin America. Rising incomes, urbanization, and changing consumer preferences in these regions are driving demand for FMCG products.

2: Middle-Class Expansion: The expanding middle class in emerging markets presents a major growth opportunity for FMCG companies. This demographic is increasingly seeking convenience, quality, and health-oriented products.

3: Rural Market Penetration: FMCG companies are increasingly focusing on penetrating rural markets in emerging economies, where there is untapped potential for growth. Companies are adapting their products and distribution strategies to cater to the unique needs of rural consumers.

4: E-commerce Expansion: E-commerce is expected to play a significant role in the growth of the FMCG industry, particularly in emerging markets where access to traditional retail outlets may be limited. Companies are investing in e-commerce platforms and digital marketing to reach a wider audience.

B: Technological Advancements Shaping the Industry

1: Digital Transformation: The FMCG industry is undergoing a digital transformation, with companies adopting digital technologies such as big data analytics, artificial intelligence (AI), and Internet of Things (IoT) to improve operational efficiency, enhance customer engagement, and drive innovation.

2: Personalization: Technology is enabling FMCG companies to personalize their products and services to meet the specific needs and preferences of individual consumers. This includes offering customized products, personalized recommendations, and targeted marketing campaigns.

3: Supply Chain Optimization: Technology is helping FMCG companies optimize their supply chains, reduce costs, and improve efficiency. Advanced analytics and automation are being used to streamline logistics, inventory management, and production processes.

4: Sustainable Practices: Technology is enabling FMCG companies to adopt more sustainable practices, such as using renewable energy sources, reducing waste, and implementing eco-friendly packaging solutions. Consumers are increasingly demanding environmentally friendly products, driving companies to innovate in this area.

5: Direct-to-Consumer (DTC) Models: Technology is facilitating the growth of DTC models in the FMCG industry, allowing companies to bypass traditional retail channels and sell directly to consumers. This enables companies to have more control over their brand and customer relationships.

Overall, the future outlook for the FMCG industry is promising, with opportunities for growth in emerging markets and advancements in technology driving innovation and efficiency. Companies that are able to adapt to these changes and embrace new opportunities are likely to succeed in the evolving FMCG landscape.

Chapter 16: Digital Transformation in FMCG

A: Adoption of Digital Technologies in Marketing, Sales, and Operations

1: Marketing: FMCG companies are increasingly using digital technologies such as social media, search engine optimization (SEO), and online advertising to reach consumers. Digital marketing allows companies to target specific demographics, track campaign performance, and engage with consumers in real-time.

2: Sales: Digital technologies are transforming the way FMCG companies sell their products. E-commerce platforms allow companies to sell directly to consumers, bypassing traditional retail channels. Mobile apps and online marketplaces are also being used to facilitate sales and improve customer convenience.

3: Operations: Digital technologies are streamlining FMCG operations, making them more efficient and cost-effective. Supply chain management systems use data analytics and automation to optimize inventory management, reduce waste, and improve logistics. Manufacturing processes are also being digitized, with the adoption of robotics and smart technologies to improve production efficiency.

B: Impact of Data Analytics and AI on FMCG Companies

1: Data Analytics: Data analytics is helping FMCG companies gain valuable insights into consumer behavior, market trends, and operational performance. By analyzing large volumes of data, companies can make informed decisions, identify opportunities for growth, and optimize their marketing and sales strategies.

2: AI and Machine Learning: AI and machine learning are revolutionizing the FMCG industry, enabling companies to automate processes, personalize marketing campaigns, and enhance product development. AI-powered tools can analyze consumer data to predict trends, forecast demand, and recommend product innovations.

3: Personalization: Data analytics and AI are enabling FMCG companies to personalize their products and services to meet the specific needs and preferences of individual consumers. Personalized marketing campaigns, product recommendations, and pricing strategies are driving customer engagement and loyalty.

4: Supply Chain Optimization: Data analytics and AI are helping FMCG companies optimize their supply chains, improving efficiency and reducing costs. AI algorithms can analyze supply chain data in real-time to identify bottlenecks, predict demand, and optimize inventory levels.

5: Customer Insights: Data analytics and AI are providing FMCG companies with deeper insights into their customers, allowing them to tailor their products and marketing strategies to better meet customer needs. By understanding customer preferences and behaviors, companies can improve customer satisfaction and loyalty.

Overall, digital transformation is reshaping the FMCG industry, enabling companies to improve their marketing, sales, and operations through the adoption of digital technologies. Companies that embrace digital transformation are likely to gain a competitive edge and succeed in the fast-paced and evolving FMCG landscape.

Chapter 17: Cross-border Expansion Strategies

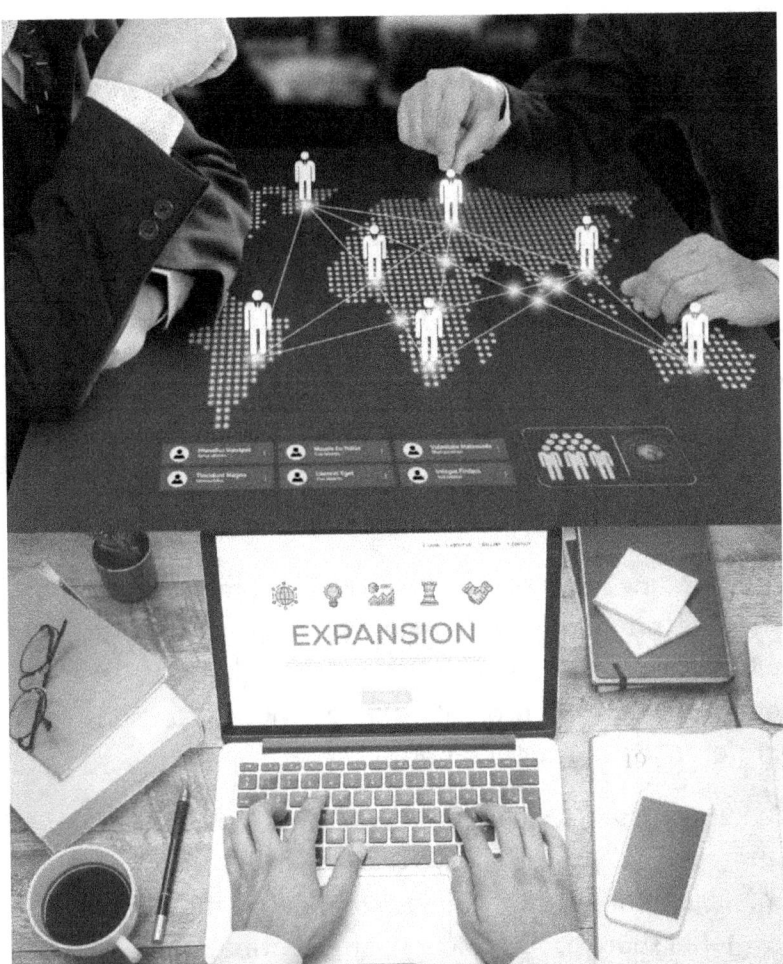

A: Internationalization Strategies for FMCG Companies

1: Market Entry Modes: FMCG companies can choose from several market entry modes when expanding internationally, including exporting, licensing, franchising, joint ventures, and wholly-owned subsidiaries. The choice of entry mode depends on factors such as market characteristics, regulatory environment, and company resources.

2: Adaptation vs. Standardization: FMCG companies must decide whether to adapt their products and marketing strategies to local markets or maintain a standardized approach. Adaptation allows companies to better meet local preferences and regulatory requirements, while standardization can lead to cost savings and brand consistency.

3: Distribution Channels: FMCG companies must establish efficient distribution channels in new markets to ensure their products reach consumers. This may involve working with local distributors, retailers, or e-commerce platforms.

4: Branding and Marketing: FMCG companies need to develop branding and marketing strategies that resonate with local consumers. This may involve adapting packaging, messaging, and promotional activities to suit local preferences and cultural norms.

5: Supply Chain Management: FMCG companies expanding internationally must ensure they have robust supply chain management practices in place to manage the complexities of global sourcing, production, and distribution.

B: Challenges and Opportunities in Entering New Markets

1: Cultural Differences: FMCG companies face the challenge of understanding and adapting to cultural differences in new markets. This includes differences in consumer preferences, buying behavior, and communication styles.

2: Regulatory Environment: FMCG companies must navigate complex regulatory environments when entering new markets, including regulations related to product labeling, packaging, and safety standards.

3: Competition: FMCG markets are often highly competitive, with local and international players vying for market share. FMCG companies entering new markets must develop strategies to differentiate themselves and gain a competitive edge.

4: Infrastructure and Logistics: FMCG companies may encounter challenges related to infrastructure and logistics when entering new markets, including poor transportation networks, inadequate storage facilities, and unreliable supply chains.

5: Economic Factors: Economic factors such as currency fluctuations, inflation, and economic instability can impact the success of FMCG companies entering new markets. Companies must carefully assess these factors and develop strategies to mitigate risks.

Despite these challenges, entering new markets can also present significant opportunities for FMCG companies, including access to new customer segments, revenue growth, and diversification of their business. By carefully planning their international expansion strategies and addressing key challenges, FMCG companies can successfully enter and thrive in new markets.

Chapter 18: Brand Loyalty Programs

A: Importance of Loyalty Programs in FMCG

1: Customer Retention: Loyalty programs are essential for FMCG companies to retain their customers in a highly competitive market. These programs offer incentives for customers to continue purchasing from the same brand, increasing their loyalty and lifetime value.

2: Repeat Purchases: Loyalty programs encourage repeat purchases by rewarding customers for their loyalty. This helps FMCG companies maintain a steady stream of revenue and increase customer engagement.

3: Brand Advocacy: Loyalty programs can turn satisfied customers into brand advocates. Customers who are rewarded for their loyalty are more likely to recommend the brand to others, leading to word-of-mouth referrals and increased brand awareness.

4: Data Collection: Loyalty programs provide valuable data about customer preferences, buying behavior, and demographics. This data can be used to tailor marketing campaigns, improve product offerings, and enhance the overall customer experience.

5: Competitive Advantage: A well-designed loyalty program can give FMCG companies a competitive advantage by differentiating their brand from competitors. Customers are more likely to choose a brand that offers rewards and incentives for their loyalty.

B: Best Practices and Case Studies

1: Points-Based Systems: Many FMCG companies use points-based loyalty programs, where customers earn points for every purchase that can be redeemed for rewards or discounts. This encourages repeat purchases and builds customer loyalty.

2: Personalization: Personalized loyalty programs are more effective in engaging customers. FMCG companies can use data analytics to personalize offers and rewards based on individual customer preferences and behavior.

3: Mobile Integration: Mobile apps are increasingly used to enhance loyalty programs, allowing customers to easily track their points, redeem rewards, and receive personalized offers. This improves the customer experience and encourages engagement.

4: Gamification: Gamification techniques, such as challenges, badges, and leaderboards, can make loyalty programs more engaging and fun for customers. This can increase participation and loyalty.

5: Case Studies:

a: Starbucks Rewards: Starbucks Rewards is a successful loyalty program that offers customers points for every purchase, which can be redeemed for free drinks and food items. The program has helped Starbucks increase customer retention and engagement.

b: Sephora Beauty Insider: Sephora's Beauty Insider program offers customers rewards, exclusive offers, and personalized experiences based on their purchase history. The program has helped Sephora build a loyal customer base and increase sales.

In conclusion, loyalty programs are a valuable tool for FMCG companies to increase customer retention, encourage repeat purchases, and build brand advocacy. By implementing best practices and learning from successful case studies, FMCG companies can create effective loyalty programs that drive customer engagement and loyalty.

Chapter 19: Crisis Management in FMCG

A: Strategies for Managing Product Recalls and Other Crises

1: Rapid Response: FMCG companies must respond quickly to crises such as product recalls to mitigate damage to their brand reputation. This includes identifying the issue, notifying stakeholders, and implementing corrective actions.

2: Transparency: FMCG companies should be transparent in their communications during a crisis, providing clear and accurate information to consumers, regulators, and the media. This helps build trust and credibility.

3: Recall Procedures: FMCG companies should have robust recall procedures in place to ensure the prompt and effective removal of affected products from the market. This includes identifying the scope of the recall, notifying retailers and consumers, and disposing of or correcting the products.

4: Customer Communication: FMCG companies should communicate with customers affected by a recall, providing clear instructions on how to return or dispose of the product and offering refunds or replacements as appropriate.

5: Regulatory Compliance: FMCG companies must comply with regulatory requirements during a crisis, including reporting the issue to regulatory authorities and cooperating with investigations.

B: Rebuilding Brand Reputation after a Crisis

1: Apologize and Take Responsibility: FMCG companies should publicly apologize for any harm caused by the crisis and take responsibility for the issue. This demonstrates accountability and a commitment to addressing the problem.

2: Implement Corrective Actions: FMCG companies should take corrective actions to prevent similar crises from occurring in the future. This may include improving quality control processes, implementing new safety measures, or revising product formulations.

3: Communicate Changes: FMCG companies should communicate the changes they have made in response to the crisis to reassure customers and stakeholders. This demonstrates a commitment to improvement and transparency.

4: Engage with Stakeholders: FMCG companies should engage with stakeholders, including customers, employees, and regulators, to rebuild trust and confidence. This may include hosting public forums, conducting surveys, and seeking feedback on new initiatives.

5: Rebuild Brand Image: FMCG companies should focus on rebuilding their brand image through positive marketing campaigns, community outreach programs, and partnerships with trusted organizations. This helps restore consumer confidence and loyalty.

In conclusion, crisis management is a critical aspect of FMCG operations, and companies must be prepared to respond effectively to product recalls and other crises. By implementing strategies for managing crises and rebuilding brand reputation, FMCG companies can minimize the impact of a crisis and emerge stronger and more resilient.

Chapter 20: Private Label Brands

A: Growth of Private Label Brands in FMCG

1: Market Share Growth: Private label brands, also known as store brands or own brands, have been steadily gaining market share in the FMCG sector. This growth is driven by factors such as improved product quality, competitive pricing, and increased consumer acceptance.

2: Retailer Focus: Retailers have been placing more emphasis on developing and promoting their private label brands as a way to differentiate themselves from competitors and increase customer loyalty. Private label brands are often positioned as high-quality alternatives to national brands at lower prices.

3: Consumer Perception: Consumer perception of private label brands has shifted in recent years, with many consumers now viewing them as comparable in quality to national brands. This change in perception has been driven by improved product formulations, packaging, and marketing strategies.

4: Category Expansion: Private label brands are expanding beyond traditional FMCG categories such as food and household products into categories such as beauty, personal care, and health products. This expansion is driven by consumer demand for value and quality across a wider range of products.

B: Strategies for Competing with Private Labels

1: Differentiation: FMCG companies can differentiate their products from private label brands by focusing on unique product features, innovative formulations, and superior packaging. This can help attract customers who are willing to pay a premium for these attributes.

2: Branding and Marketing: FMCG companies should invest in branding and marketing strategies to build brand awareness and loyalty. Effective branding can help create a strong emotional connection with consumers, making them less likely to switch to private label brands.

3: Product Innovation: FMCG companies should focus on product innovation to stay ahead of private label brands. This may include developing new formulations, flavors, or packaging formats that offer unique benefits to consumers.

4: Pricing Strategies: FMCG companies should carefully consider their pricing strategies to remain competitive with private label brands. This may involve offering promotional pricing, bundle deals, or loyalty programs to attract and retain customers.

5: Distribution Channels: FMCG companies should ensure their products are available in a wide range of distribution channels to reach as many consumers as possible. This may include traditional retail outlets, online platforms, and specialty stores.

By implementing these strategies, FMCG companies can effectively compete with private label brands and maintain their market share and profitability in the face of increasing competition.

Chapter 21: Direct-to-Consumer (DTC) Trends

A: Rise of DTC Models in FMCG

1: Changing Consumer Behavior: Consumer preferences are shifting towards convenience and personalized shopping experiences, driving the demand for DTC models in the FMCG sector. Consumers are increasingly looking for direct access to brands, bypassing traditional retail channels.

2: Digital Transformation: The digital transformation of the FMCG industry has enabled DTC models to flourish. E-commerce platforms, social media, and digital marketing have made it easier for FMCG companies to reach consumers directly and establish DTC channels.

3: Brand Control: DTC models allow FMCG companies to have more control over their brand image, messaging, and customer interactions. This can lead to stronger brand loyalty and higher customer lifetime value.

4: Data Insights: DTC models provide FMCG companies with valuable data insights into consumer behavior, preferences, and purchasing habits. This data can be used to personalize marketing efforts, improve product offerings, and enhance the overall customer experience.

B: Benefits and Challenges of Selling Directly to Consumers

1: Benefits:

a: Increased Profit Margins: By selling directly to consumers, FMCG companies can eliminate the costs associated with traditional retail channels, such as distribution, marketing, and retailer margins, leading to higher profit margins.

b: Greater Brand Control: DTC models allow FMCG companies to control their brand image, messaging, and customer interactions, leading to stronger brand loyalty and customer relationships.

c: Data Insights: DTC models provide FMCG companies with valuable data insights into consumer behavior, preferences, and purchasing habits, which can be used to personalize marketing efforts and improve product offerings.

2: Challenges:

a: Logistics and Fulfillment: FMCG companies must invest in efficient logistics and fulfillment operations to ensure timely delivery of products to customers, which can be challenging and costly.

b: Customer Acquisition: Acquiring and retaining customers in a crowded online marketplace can be challenging, requiring FMCG companies to invest in digital marketing and customer engagement strategies.

c: Regulatory Compliance: FMCG companies must comply with regulations related to online sales, data privacy, and product safety, which can vary across different markets and jurisdictions.

In conclusion, DTC models are reshaping the FMCG industry, offering FMCG companies opportunities to increase profit margins, strengthen brand loyalty, and gain valuable data insights. However, FMCG companies must also navigate challenges such as logistics, customer acquisition, and regulatory compliance to succeed in the DTC space.

Chapter 22: Mergers and Acquisitions in FMCG

A: Trends and Drivers of M&A Activity in FMCG

1: Market Consolidation: Mergers and acquisitions (M&A) are common in the FMCG sector as companies seek to consolidate their market position and gain a competitive edge. M&A activity in FMCG is often driven by the desire to expand product portfolios, enter new markets, or achieve cost efficiencies through economies of scale.

2: Innovation and Diversification: M&A can help FMCG companies acquire new technologies, products, or brands, allowing them to innovate and diversify their offerings. This can help companies stay ahead of changing consumer preferences and market trends.

3: Market Expansion: M&A can be used by FMCG companies to expand into new geographic markets or strengthen their presence in existing markets. This can help companies tap into new customer segments and distribution channels.

4: Cost Reduction: M&A can help FMCG companies achieve cost reductions through economies of scale, improved purchasing power, and streamlined operations. This can lead to increased profitability and shareholder value.

5: Strategic Partnerships: M&A can also be driven by the desire to form strategic partnerships or alliances with other companies in the FMCG sector. This can help companies leverage each other's strengths and resources to achieve common goals.

B: Case Studies of Successful and Failed Acquisitions

1: Successful Acquisition: The acquisition of Ben & Jerry's by Unilever in 2000 is often cited as a successful acquisition in the FMCG sector. Unilever's acquisition of the ice cream company allowed it to enter the premium ice cream market and leverage Ben & Jerry's strong brand image and loyal customer base.

2: Failed Acquisition: The acquisition of Quaker Oats by PepsiCo in 2001 is considered a failed acquisition in the FMCG sector. PepsiCo paid a high price for Quaker Oats, expecting to benefit from its popular brands such as Gatorade and Quaker Oats. However, integration challenges and declining sales of Quaker Oats products led to the acquisition being deemed unsuccessful.

3: Successful Acquisition: The acquisition of Whole Foods Market by Amazon in 2017 is another successful acquisition in the FMCG sector. Amazon's acquisition of the grocery chain allowed it to enter the brick-and-mortar retail market and expand its presence in the food and beverage sector.

4: Failed Acquisition: The acquisition of Cadbury by Kraft Foods in 2010 is considered a failed acquisition in the FMCG sector. Kraft Foods faced backlash from Cadbury's employees, customers, and shareholders due to concerns about job losses and changes to the Cadbury brand. This led to a decline in sales and profitability for Kraft Foods following the acquisition.

In conclusion, M&A activity in the FMCG sector is driven by various factors such as market consolidation, innovation, and market expansion. While some acquisitions have been successful in helping companies achieve their strategic objectives, others have failed due to integration challenges, cultural differences, or other factors. Successful M&A in the FMCG sector requires careful planning, due diligence, and a clear strategic vision.

Chapter 23: Social Media Marketing in FMCG

A: Impact of Social Media on FMCG Marketing

1: Increased Reach: Social media platforms allow FMCG companies to reach a large audience of consumers, including those who may not be reached through traditional marketing channels. This increased reach can help companies build brand awareness and attract new customers.

2: Customer Engagement: Social media enables FMCG companies to engage directly with consumers in real-time, allowing for more personalized interactions and customer feedback. This can help companies build stronger relationships with their customers and increase brand loyalty.

3: Targeted Advertising: Social media platforms offer advanced targeting options that allow FMCG companies to reach specific demographics, interests, and behaviors. This targeted advertising can lead to higher conversion rates and more effective marketing campaigns.

4: Brand Advocacy: Social media allows satisfied customers to share their experiences with FMCG products, leading to word-of-mouth recommendations and brand advocacy. This can help companies increase their brand reputation and credibility.

5: Data Analytics: Social media provides FMCG companies with valuable data insights into consumer behavior, preferences, and trends. This data can be used to optimize marketing strategies, improve product offerings, and enhance the overall customer experience.

B: Best Practices for Engaging Consumers on Social Platforms

1: Consistent Branding: FMCG companies should maintain consistent branding across all social media platforms to ensure a cohesive brand identity and message.

2: Visual Content: Visual content such as images and videos perform well on social media and can help FMCG companies showcase their products in an engaging way.

3: Customer Engagement: FMCG companies should actively engage with their followers on social media by responding to comments, messages, and mentions. This can help build relationships with customers and increase brand loyalty.

4: Influencer Partnerships: Collaborating with influencers and bloggers can help FMCG companies reach a larger audience and gain credibility among consumers.

5: Contests and Giveaways: Hosting contests and giveaways on social media can help FMCG companies increase engagement and reach new customers.

6: Analytics and Monitoring: FMCG companies should regularly monitor social media metrics such as engagement rates, reach, and sentiment to track the performance of their campaigns and make adjustments as needed.

Overall, social media marketing has become an integral part of FMCG marketing strategies, offering companies new opportunities to reach and engage with consumers. By leveraging the power of social media, FMCG companies can increase brand awareness, build customer loyalty, and drive sales.

Chapter 24: Health and Wellness Trends

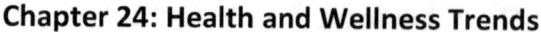

A: Consumer Demand for Healthier and Natural Products

1: Increased Awareness: Consumers are becoming more aware of the importance of health and wellness, leading to a growing demand for products that are perceived as healthier and more natural.

2: Transparency: Consumers are seeking transparency in food and product labeling, looking for clear and understandable information about ingredients, sourcing, and manufacturing processes.

3: Clean Label Movement: The clean label movement emphasizes the use of simple, natural ingredients and the avoidance of artificial additives, preservatives, and chemicals in food and products.

4: Functional Foods: Functional foods are products that provide additional health benefits beyond basic nutrition. These products often contain ingredients such as vitamins, minerals, antioxidants, or probiotics.

5: Personalization: Consumers are increasingly seeking personalized health and wellness solutions, including personalized nutrition plans, fitness programs, and beauty products.

B: Strategies for Developing and Marketing Health-focused FMCG Products

1: Research and Development: FMCG companies should invest in research and development to create products that meet consumer demand for healthier and more natural options. This may involve reformulating existing products or developing new products that align with health and wellness trends.

2: Clean Labeling: FMCG companies should prioritize clean labeling by using simple, natural ingredients and avoiding artificial additives, preservatives, and chemicals. Clear and transparent labeling can help build trust with consumers.

3: Health Claims: FMCG companies should use health claims and certifications to highlight the health benefits of their products. This can include claims related to nutrition, ingredients, and production methods.

4: Marketing and Advertising: FMCG companies should use marketing and advertising strategies that resonate with health-conscious consumers. This may include highlighting the natural and organic ingredients, the health benefits of the product, and the company's commitment to sustainability and ethical practices.

5: Partnerships and Collaborations: FMCG companies can partner with health and wellness experts, influencers, and organizations to promote their products and reach a wider audience of health-conscious consumers.

6: Innovation: FMCG companies should continuously innovate to stay ahead of health and wellness trends. This may involve developing new products, flavors, or packaging formats that appeal to health-conscious consumers.

In conclusion, health and wellness trends are driving consumer demand for healthier and more natural FMCG products. By understanding these trends and implementing strategies to develop and market health-focused products, FMCG companies can capitalize on this growing market segment and meet the evolving needs of health-conscious consumers.

Chapter 25: Packaging Innovations

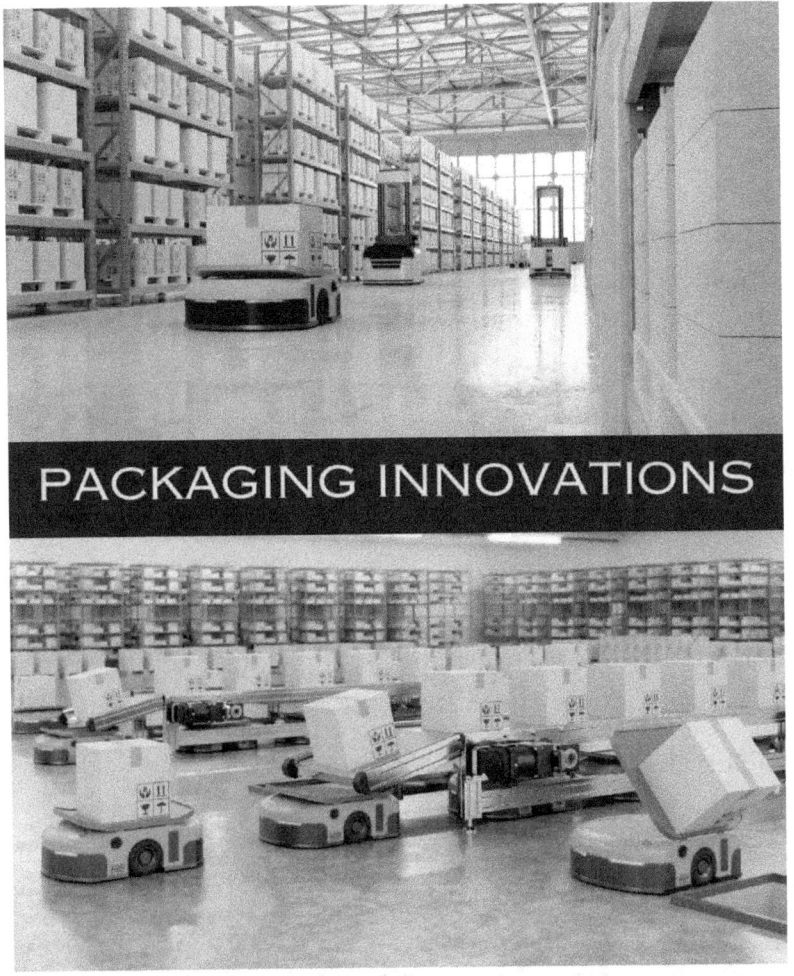

A: Latest Trends in Packaging Materials and Designs

1: Sustainable Materials: There is a growing trend towards using sustainable packaging materials, such as biodegradable plastics, recycled paper, and compostable materials, to reduce environmental impact.

2: Minimalist Design: Minimalist packaging design, characterized by clean lines, simple typography, and limited use of colors, is becoming increasingly popular as consumers seek out products that convey a sense of simplicity and authenticity.

3: Smart Packaging: Smart packaging incorporates technology, such as QR codes, RFID tags, and sensors, to provide consumers with information about the product, including origin, ingredients, and expiration date.

4: Flexible Packaging: Flexible packaging, such as pouches and sachets, is gaining popularity due to its lightweight, convenient, and cost-effective nature. It also offers opportunities for innovative designs and branding.

5: Personalized Packaging: Personalized packaging allows companies to tailor their packaging to individual consumers, such as including a customer's name or a personalized message on the package.

B: Sustainable Packaging Solutions

1: Reduce, Reuse, Recycle: FMCG companies can reduce packaging waste by using less material, designing packaging that is easy to reuse, and encouraging consumers to recycle.

2: Biodegradable and Compostable Materials: FMCG companies can use biodegradable and compostable materials for their packaging to reduce environmental impact and promote sustainability.

3: Eco-Friendly Inks and Coatings: FMCG companies can use eco-friendly inks and coatings for their packaging to minimize environmental impact and improve recyclability.

4: Lightweight Packaging: FMCG companies can reduce the weight of their packaging to minimize material use and transportation costs, which can also reduce carbon emissions.

5: Extended Producer Responsibility (EPR): FMCG companies can take responsibility for the entire lifecycle of their packaging by implementing EPR programs, which involve designing packaging for easy recycling and providing recycling facilities for consumers.

In conclusion, packaging innovations in the FMCG sector are driven by a growing focus on sustainability, convenience, and consumer engagement. By adopting sustainable packaging solutions and embracing innovative designs and materials, FMCG companies can meet consumer expectations, reduce environmental impact, and differentiate their products in the market.

Chapter 26: Retailer Relationships

A: Importance of Partnerships with Retailers in FMCG

1: Distribution Channel: Retailers play a crucial role as a distribution channel for FMCG products, providing access to a wide customer base and physical shelf space.

2: Brand Visibility: Retailers can help FMCG companies increase brand visibility and awareness by featuring their products prominently in stores and in marketing campaigns.

3: Market Insights: Retailers can provide valuable market insights to FMCG companies, such as consumer preferences, buying behavior, and competitive trends, which can help companies tailor their products and marketing strategies.

4: Promotional Opportunities: Retailers offer promotional opportunities, such as in-store displays, discounts, and promotions, which can help FMCG companies attract customers and drive sales.

5: Mutual Growth: Strong partnerships with retailers can lead to mutual growth and success, as both parties work together to meet customer needs and achieve common business goals.

B: Strategies for Maintaining Strong Retailer Relationships

1: Communication: Regular communication is key to maintaining strong retailer relationships. FMCG companies should keep retailers informed about new products, promotions, and market developments.

2: Collaboration: FMCG companies should collaborate with retailers on joint marketing initiatives, promotions, and product placements to drive sales and increase brand visibility.

3: Customer Focus: FMCG companies should focus on meeting the needs and expectations of retailers' customers, as this can help strengthen the relationship and build loyalty.

4: Flexibility: FMCG companies should be flexible and willing to adapt to retailers' needs and requirements, whether it be in terms of product assortment, pricing, or promotional strategies.

5: Performance Evaluation: FMCG companies should regularly evaluate their performance in terms of sales, distribution, and customer satisfaction, and work with retailers to identify areas for improvement.

6: Innovation: FMCG companies should continue to innovate and introduce new products and marketing strategies to keep retailers and their customers engaged and excited about their brand.

In conclusion, strong partnerships with retailers are essential for FMCG companies to succeed in the market. By prioritizing communication, collaboration, and customer focus, FMCG companies can maintain strong retailer relationships and drive mutual growth and success.

Chapter 27: Crisis Communication

A: Communicating Effectively During a Crisis

1: Immediate Response: It is essential to respond to a crisis promptly and transparently. Acknowledge the issue, take responsibility, and provide clear and accurate information to stakeholders.

2: Transparency: Be transparent in your communication during a crisis. Provide regular updates and be honest about the situation, including any mistakes that were made and the steps being taken to address the issue.

3: Empathy: Show empathy towards those affected by the crisis, including customers, employees, and other stakeholders. Acknowledge their concerns and demonstrate that you are taking their feedback seriously.

4: Consistency: Ensure that your messaging is consistent across all communication channels. This helps build trust and avoids confusion among stakeholders.

5: Accessibility: Make sure that your communication is accessible to all stakeholders, including those with disabilities or language barriers. Provide information in multiple formats if necessary.

6: Media Relations: Work closely with the media to ensure that accurate information is being reported. Provide regular updates and be available to answer questions from journalists.

B: Building and Maintaining Trust with Consumers

1: Transparency: Transparency is key to building trust with consumers. Be open and honest about your products, services, and business practices.

2: Consistency: Consistency in your messaging and actions helps build trust with consumers. Ensure that your brand values are reflected in everything you do.

3: Customer Engagement: Engage with your customers regularly through social media, email, and other channels. Listen to their feedback and respond promptly to their concerns.

4: Quality Products and Services: Providing high-quality products and services helps build trust with consumers. Ensure that your products meet or exceed industry standards and that your customer service is top-notch.

5: Ethical Business Practices: Conduct your business in an ethical and responsible manner. This includes being transparent about your sourcing and manufacturing practices and treating your employees and partners fairly.

6: Crisis Preparedness: Being prepared for a crisis can help you respond more effectively and maintain trust with consumers. Develop a crisis communication plan and regularly review and update it as needed.

By communicating effectively during a crisis and building and maintaining trust with consumers, FMCG companies can protect their reputation and maintain strong relationships with stakeholders.

Chapter 28: Pricing Strategies

A: Pricing Strategies for Different FMCG Categories

1: Penetration Pricing: This strategy involves setting a low price to enter a competitive market and attract customers. Once a customer base is established, prices may be gradually increased.

2: Price Skimming: Price skimming involves setting a high initial price for a new product and then gradually lowering the price over time. This strategy is often used for innovative products with unique features.

3: Premium Pricing: Premium pricing involves setting a high price to reflect the quality or exclusivity of a product. This strategy is often used for luxury FMCG products.

4: Economy Pricing: Economy pricing involves setting a low price to attract price-sensitive customers. This strategy is often used for basic, no-frills products.

5: Bundle Pricing: Bundle pricing involves offering multiple products or services for a lower price than if they were purchased separately. This strategy can encourage customers to buy more products.

6: Psychological Pricing: Psychological pricing involves setting prices that appeal to customers' emotions or perceptions. For example, setting prices at $9.99 instead of $10 can make the product seem more affordable.

B: Dynamic Pricing and Price Optimization Techniques

1: Dynamic Pricing: Dynamic pricing involves adjusting prices in real-time based on factors such as demand, competitor pricing, and inventory levels. This strategy is often used in e-commerce and can help maximize revenue.

2: Price Optimization: Price optimization involves using data analytics and algorithms to determine the optimal price for a product based on factors such as demand, customer behavior, and market conditions. This can help FMCG companies maximize profits and sales volume.

3: Price Discrimination: Price discrimination involves charging different prices to different customer segments based on their willingness to pay. This strategy is often used in industries such as airlines and hotels.

4: Promotional Pricing: Promotional pricing involves offering discounts or special offers for a limited time to stimulate sales. This strategy can help FMCG companies attract new customers and increase sales volume.

5: Value-Based Pricing: Value-based pricing involves setting prices based on the perceived value of a product to the customer. This strategy considers factors such as the benefits of the product, the customer's alternatives, and the customer's willingness to pay.

By implementing these pricing strategies and techniques, FMCG companies can effectively manage their pricing strategy and maximize revenue and profitability.

Chapter 29: Product Life Cycle Management

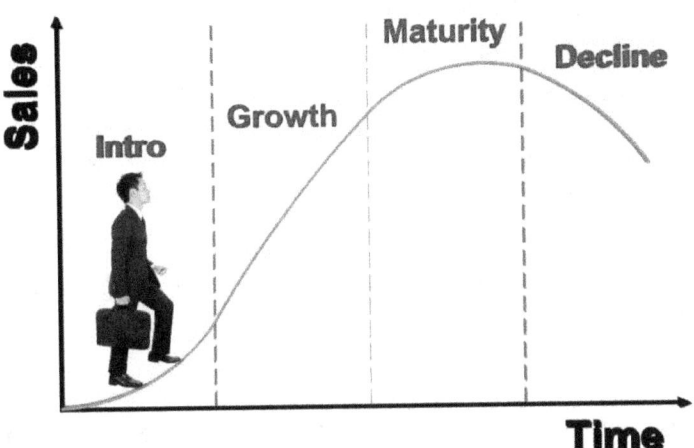

A: Strategies for Managing Products Through Different Stages of the Life Cycle

1: Introduction Stage: During the introduction stage, focus on building awareness and establishing a market for the product. Pricing strategies may vary, such as price skimming or penetration pricing, depending on market conditions and competitive landscape.

2: Growth Stage: In the growth stage, focus on expanding market share and maximizing sales. Consider product line extensions, entering new markets, and increasing distribution channels. Pricing strategies may become more competitive as competitors enter the market.

3: Maturity Stage: In the maturity stage, sales growth slows down as the market becomes saturated. Focus on maintaining market share through product differentiation, cost leadership, or marketing campaigns. Pricing strategies may include discounts, promotions, or bundling to maintain sales.

4: Decline Stage: In the decline stage, sales and profits decline as the product becomes obsolete or faces strong competition. Consider discontinuing the product or offering it to niche markets. Pricing strategies may involve reducing prices to liquidate remaining inventory.

B: Revitalizing Mature Products

1: Product Innovation: Introduce new features, formulations, or packaging to make the product more attractive to consumers. This can help rejuvenate interest in the product and extend its life cycle.

2: Repositioning: Reposition the product to appeal to new or different market segments. This may involve updating the brand image, marketing message, or distribution channels.

3: Pricing Strategies: Consider adjusting pricing strategies to make the product more competitive. This may involve offering discounts, promotions, or bundle deals to attract price-sensitive consumers.

4: Marketing Campaigns: Launch targeted marketing campaigns to re-engage existing customers and attract new ones. Highlight the product's unique features or benefits to differentiate it from competitors.

5: Strategic Partnerships: Form partnerships with other companies or brands to create co-branded products or exclusive offerings. This can help generate excitement and interest in the product.

By effectively managing products through different stages of the life cycle and implementing strategies to revitalize mature products, FMCG companies can maximize the potential of their product portfolio and maintain competitiveness in the market.

Chapter 30: E-commerce Strategies

A: Strategies for Selling FMCG Products Online

1: Establishing a Strong Online Presence: Create a user-friendly website or mobile app where customers can easily browse and purchase your FMCG products. Optimize your website for search engines to increase visibility.

2: Leveraging E-commerce Platforms: Utilize popular e-commerce platforms such as Amazon, Alibaba, or eBay to reach a wider audience and benefit from their established customer base and logistics infrastructure.

3: Digital Marketing: Implement digital marketing strategies such as search engine optimization (SEO), pay-per-click (PPC) advertising, and social media marketing to drive traffic to your online store and increase sales.

4: Omnichannel Retailing: Integrate your online and offline sales channels to provide a seamless shopping experience for customers. Allow customers to purchase online and pick up in-store, or vice versa.

5: Personalization: Use customer data and analytics to personalize the shopping experience for each customer. Offer personalized product recommendations, discounts, and promotions based on their browsing and purchasing history.

6: Customer Engagement: Engage with customers through email marketing, social media, and other channels to build relationships and encourage repeat purchases. Offer loyalty programs and special discounts for returning customers.

B: Fulfillment and Delivery Challenges in E-commerce

1: Inventory Management: Efficient inventory management is crucial in e-commerce to avoid stockouts or overstocking. Use inventory management software to track inventory levels and forecast demand accurately.

2: Order Fulfillment: Streamline the order fulfillment process to ensure orders are processed and shipped quickly and accurately. Consider outsourcing fulfillment to third-party logistics providers (3PLs) to reduce costs and improve efficiency.

3: Shipping Costs: Shipping costs can significantly impact the profitability of e-commerce sales. Negotiate favorable shipping rates with carriers and consider offering free shipping thresholds to incentivize larger orders.

4: Last-Mile Delivery: Last-mile delivery is often the most expensive and challenging part of the delivery process. Consider using local delivery partners or implementing click-and-collect options to reduce costs and improve delivery times.

5: Returns Management: Develop a streamlined returns process to handle returns efficiently and minimize the impact on your business. Provide clear return policies and instructions to customers to reduce confusion and friction.

By implementing these strategies and addressing fulfillment and delivery challenges, FMCG companies can effectively sell their products online and capitalize on the growing e-commerce market.

Chapter 31: Rural Marketing

A: Strategies for Reaching Consumers in Rural Areas

1: Understanding the Rural Market: Conduct thorough market research to understand the needs, preferences, and buying behavior of consumers in rural areas. Factors such as income levels, infrastructure, and cultural nuances should be considered.

2: Distribution Network: Establish a robust distribution network that reaches deep into rural areas. Utilize local retailers, cooperatives, and self-help groups to ensure widespread availability of your products.

3: Affordable Pricing: Offer products at affordable prices that cater to the purchasing power of rural consumers. Consider offering smaller pack sizes or sachets to make products more accessible.

4: Product Localization: Adapt your products to suit the needs and preferences of rural consumers. This may include adjusting product formulations, sizes, or packaging to better align with local preferences.

5: Promotional Strategies: Utilize local media channels such as radio, newspapers, and community events to promote your products. Engage with local influencers and community leaders to build trust and credibility.

6: After-Sales Service: Provide reliable after-sales service and support to rural consumers. This can help build loyalty and encourage repeat purchases.

B: Adapting Products and Marketing Campaigns for Rural Markets

1: Language and Communication: Use local languages and dialects in your marketing campaigns to effectively communicate with rural consumers. Avoid jargon and use simple, easy-to-understand messaging.

2: Cultural Sensitivity: Be mindful of local customs, traditions, and taboos when designing marketing campaigns. Respect local culture and values to avoid alienating potential customers.

3: Product Packaging: Consider adapting product packaging to better suit rural environments. Use durable materials that can withstand rough handling and extreme weather conditions.

4: Brand Positioning: Position your brand as a solution to the specific needs and challenges faced by rural consumers. Highlight how your products can improve their quality of life and meet their unique requirements.

5: Engaging Community Influencers: Work with local influencers, community leaders, and opinion makers to promote your products. Their endorsement can help build trust and credibility among rural consumers.

6: Education and Awareness: Educate rural consumers about the benefits and uses of your products through demonstrations, workshops, and other educational initiatives. This can help overcome any skepticism or lack of awareness about your products.

By implementing these strategies and adapting products and marketing campaigns for rural markets, FMCG companies can effectively reach and engage with rural consumers, tap into this large and growing market segment, and drive sales and growth.

Chapter 32: Corporate Social Responsibility (CSR) in FMCG

A: Importance of CSR for FMCG Companies

1: Brand Reputation: CSR initiatives can enhance a company's reputation and brand image, making it more attractive to consumers, investors, and employees.

2: Stakeholder Engagement: CSR helps companies engage with stakeholders such as customers, employees, suppliers, and communities, building trust and loyalty.

3: Risk Management: CSR can help mitigate risks related to environmental, social, and governance issues, reducing potential legal, financial, and reputational risks.

4: License to Operate: CSR is increasingly seen as a requirement for companies to maintain their social license to operate, especially in industries with significant social and environmental impacts.

5: Innovation and Differentiation: CSR can drive innovation and help companies differentiate their products and services in the market.

B: CSR Initiatives and Their Impact on Brand Image

1: Environmental Sustainability: FMCG companies can implement initiatives to reduce their environmental footprint, such as using sustainable sourcing, reducing waste, and improving energy efficiency. These initiatives can enhance their brand image as environmentally responsible companies.

2: Social Welfare Programs: FMCG companies can support social welfare programs such as education, healthcare, and poverty alleviation in the communities where they operate. These initiatives can improve their brand image as socially responsible companies that care about the well-being of society.

3: Ethical Sourcing Practices: FMCG companies can ensure ethical sourcing practices, such as fair trade and labor standards, to improve their brand image as companies that value ethical business practices.

4: Employee Engagement: FMCG companies can implement employee engagement programs, such as volunteer opportunities and diversity and inclusion initiatives, to enhance their brand image as employers of choice that care about their employees' well-being.

5: Transparency and Reporting: FMCG companies can demonstrate their commitment to CSR through transparent reporting on their CSR initiatives and impacts. This can improve their brand image as transparent and accountable companies.

Overall, CSR is an important aspect of business strategy for FMCG companies, as it can help enhance brand image, engage stakeholders, mitigate risks, and drive innovation and differentiation. By implementing meaningful CSR initiatives, FMCG companies can create long-term value for society and their business.

Chapter 33: Trade Promotion Management

A: Strategies for Managing Trade Promotions

1: Clear Objectives: Define clear objectives for trade promotions, such as increasing sales volume, gaining market share, or promoting new products. Align these objectives with overall business goals.

2: Promotion Planning: Plan trade promotions carefully, taking into account factors such as timing, duration, promotion type (e.g., discounts, coupons, displays), and targeted customer segments.

3: Budget Allocation: Allocate a budget for trade promotions based on their expected impact on sales and profitability. Monitor spending closely to ensure it stays within budget.

4: Collaboration with Retailers: Collaborate closely with retailers to plan and execute trade promotions effectively. Understand their needs and preferences to create mutually beneficial promotions.

5: Monitoring and Evaluation: Monitor the performance of trade promotions regularly against predefined KPIs, such as sales lift, ROI, and incremental volume. Evaluate the effectiveness of each promotion to inform future decisions.

6: Continuous Improvement: Continuously review and refine trade promotion strategies based on performance data and market feedback. Experiment with new approaches to optimize results.

B: Measuring the Effectiveness of Trade Promotions

1: Sales Lift: Measure the impact of trade promotions on sales volume compared to baseline sales. Calculate the incremental sales generated by the promotion to determine its effectiveness.

2: ROI Analysis: Calculate the return on investment (ROI) for each trade promotion by comparing the cost of the promotion to the additional revenue generated. This helps determine the profitability of the promotion.

3: Market Share: Monitor changes in market share during and after trade promotions to assess their impact on competitive positioning.

4: Customer Acquisition and Retention: Track the acquisition of new customers and the retention of existing customers as a result of trade promotions. This helps determine their long-term impact on customer loyalty.

5: Brand Awareness and Perception: Measure changes in brand awareness and perception resulting from trade promotions. This can include surveys, social media sentiment analysis, and other feedback mechanisms.

6: Distribution and Shelf Presence: Monitor changes in product distribution and shelf presence resulting from trade promotions. This can help assess their impact on visibility and availability in retail outlets.

By implementing these strategies for managing trade promotions and measuring their effectiveness, FMCG companies can optimize their promotional activities, drive sales growth, and improve overall profitability.

Chapter 34: Product Differentiation

A: Strategies for Differentiating FMCG Products in a Crowded Market

1: Unique Product Features: Develop products with unique features or innovations that set them apart from competitors. This could include new ingredients, formulations, packaging, or functionality.

2: Branding and Packaging: Create distinctive branding and packaging that make your products stand out on the shelves. Use colors, logos, and designs that resonate with your target audience and convey your brand's unique identity.

3: Product Quality: Focus on delivering high-quality products that consistently meet or exceed customer expectations. This can help build trust and loyalty among customers who value quality.

4: Pricing Strategies: Differentiate your products through pricing strategies, such as offering premium products at a higher price point or value products at a lower price point. This can appeal to different segments of the market based on their preferences and budget.

5: Targeted Marketing: Tailor your marketing efforts to specific segments of the market based on their preferences, demographics, or behavior. This can help you reach customers more effectively and differentiate your products in their eyes.

6: Product Positioning: Position your products in the market based on unique attributes or benefits that are relevant to your target audience. This can help create a distinct identity for your products in the minds of consumers.

B: Creating Unique Value Propositions

1: Identify Customer Needs: Conduct market research to identify unmet needs or pain points among your target audience. Use this information to develop products that address these needs in a unique and compelling way.

2: Highlight Benefits: Clearly communicate the benefits of your products to customers, focusing on what sets them apart from competitors. This could include superior performance, convenience, health benefits, or environmental sustainability.

3: Consistent Messaging: Ensure that your messaging is consistent across all marketing channels and aligns with your brand's unique value proposition. This helps reinforce your brand's identity and differentiation in the minds of consumers.

4: Customer Engagement: Engage with customers to gather feedback, testimonials, and reviews that highlight the unique benefits of your products. This can help build credibility and reinforce your value proposition.

5: Innovation: Continuously innovate and improve your products to stay ahead of competitors and meet evolving customer needs. This could involve introducing new features, formulations, or packaging that differentiate your products in the market.

6: Competitive Analysis: Monitor competitors' products and strategies to identify opportunities for differentiation. Look for gaps in the market where you can offer something unique and valuable to customers.

By implementing these strategies for product differentiation and creating unique value propositions, FMCG companies can stand out in a crowded market, attract customers, and build a loyal customer base.

Chapter 35: Outsourcing and Contract Manufacturing

A: Benefits and Challenges of Outsourcing in FMCG

1: Cost Savings: Outsourcing can help FMCG companies reduce costs by leveraging the lower labor and production costs of contract manufacturers.

2: Focus on Core Competencies: Outsourcing allows FMCG companies to focus on their core competencies, such as product development, marketing, and distribution, while leaving manufacturing to specialized partners.

3: Scalability: Contract manufacturing enables FMCG companies to scale production up or down quickly in response to market demand, without the need for significant capital investment.

4: Access to Expertise: Contract manufacturers often have specialized knowledge, expertise, and equipment that may not be available in-house, allowing FMCG companies to benefit from their capabilities.

5: Flexibility: Outsourcing provides FMCG companies with flexibility in production, allowing them to adapt to changing market conditions and customer preferences more easily.

6: Quality Control: Outsourcing can sometimes lead to challenges in maintaining quality control and ensuring that products meet the required standards and specifications.

7: Communication and Coordination: Managing outsourcing relationships requires effective communication and coordination between the FMCG company and the contract manufacturer, which can be challenging, especially in global supply chains.

8: Intellectual Property Protection: There may be risks associated with protecting intellectual property when outsourcing production to third parties, particularly in regions with weaker IP protection laws.

B: Best Practices for Managing Contract Manufacturing Relationships

1: Clear Communication: Maintain open and transparent communication with contract manufacturers to ensure that both parties understand expectations, timelines, and deliverables.

2: Contract Management: Clearly define the terms of the contract, including pricing, quality standards, delivery schedules, and dispute resolution mechanisms, to avoid misunderstandings and conflicts.

3: Quality Assurance: Implement robust quality assurance processes to ensure that products manufactured by third parties meet the required quality standards and specifications.

4: Relationship Building: Build strong relationships with contract manufacturers based on trust, mutual respect, and collaboration. Visit manufacturing facilities regularly and engage in face-to-face meetings to strengthen the relationship.

5: Performance Monitoring: Continuously monitor the performance of contract manufacturers against key performance indicators (KPIs) and take corrective actions as needed to ensure compliance with contractual obligations.

6: Continuous Improvement: Encourage contract manufacturers to suggest and implement process improvements that can enhance efficiency, quality, and cost-effectiveness.

7: Risk Management: Identify and mitigate risks associated with outsourcing, such as supply chain disruptions, quality issues, and intellectual property risks, through effective risk management strategies.

By following these best practices, FMCG companies can effectively manage their outsourcing and contract manufacturing relationships, maximize the benefits of outsourcing, and mitigate potential challenges.

Chapter 36: Omni-channel Retailing

A: Integrating Online and Offline Channels in FMCG Retail

1: Multi-channel Presence: FMCG companies should have a presence across multiple channels, including physical stores, e-commerce websites, mobile apps, and social media platforms.

2: Unified Brand Experience: Provide a consistent brand experience across all channels, including consistent branding, messaging, and pricing.

3: Inventory Management: Implement a centralized inventory management system to ensure that product availability and pricing are consistent across all channels.

4: Click-and-Collect: Offer a click-and-collect option that allows customers to order online and pick up their purchases in-store, providing convenience and flexibility.

5: Store Fulfillment: Use physical stores as fulfillment centers for online orders to reduce shipping times and costs.

6: Customer Data Integration: Integrate customer data from online and offline channels to provide personalized shopping experiences and targeted marketing campaigns.

B: Providing a Seamless Shopping Experience Across Channels

1: Consistent Product Information: Ensure that product information, such as descriptions, images, and pricing, is consistent across all channels to avoid confusion and maintain trust.

2: Unified Shopping Cart: Offer a unified shopping cart that allows customers to add items from different channels and complete their purchase in a single transaction.

3: Cross-Channel Promotions: Offer promotions and discounts that are available across all channels to encourage customers to shop across different channels.

4: Seamless Returns and Exchanges: Provide a seamless returns and exchanges process that allows customers to return or exchange products purchased online in-store, and vice versa.

5: Integrated Loyalty Programs: Integrate loyalty programs across all channels to reward customers for their purchases and encourage repeat business.

6: Customer Service: Provide consistent and seamless customer service across all channels, including online chat, email, and phone support, to resolve any issues or inquiries promptly.

By integrating online and offline channels and providing a seamless shopping experience across all channels, FMCG companies can enhance customer satisfaction, increase sales, and build brand loyalty.

Chapter 37: Emerging Technologies in FMCG

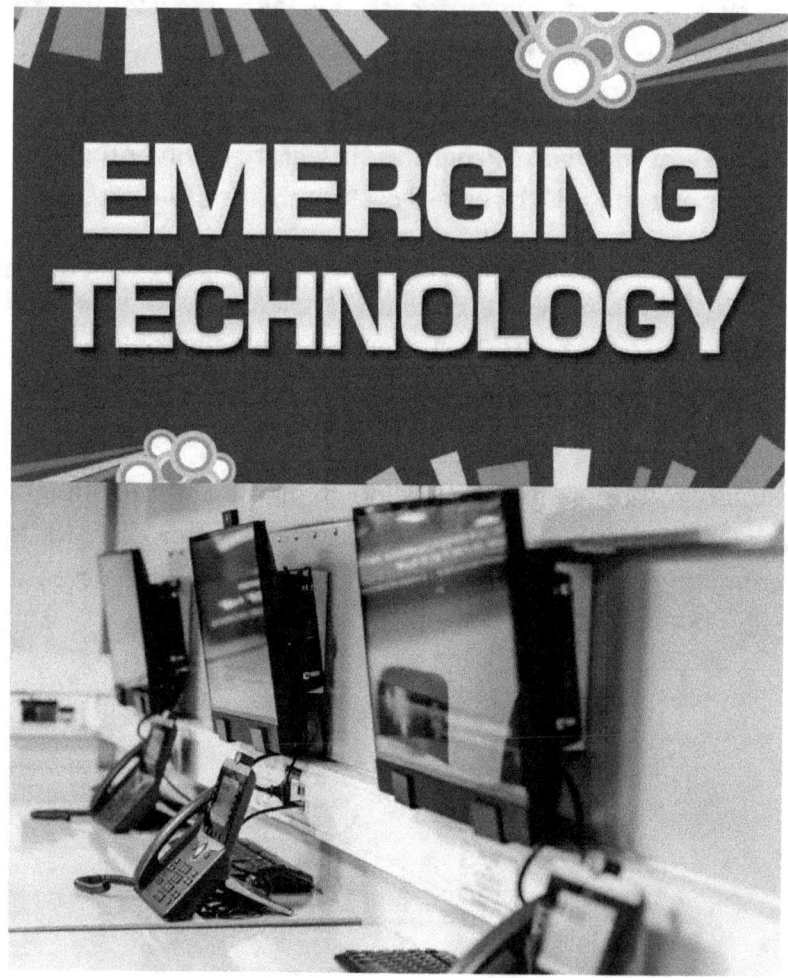

A: Role of Blockchain, IoT, and Other Technologies in FMCG

1: Blockchain: Blockchain technology can be used to create transparent and secure supply chains in the FMCG industry. It enables tracking of products from the source to the consumer, ensuring authenticity and reducing the risk of counterfeit products.

2: Internet of Things (IoT): IoT devices can be used to collect data on product usage, storage conditions, and consumer behavior. This data can be used to optimize production, distribution, and marketing strategies.

3: Artificial Intelligence (AI): AI can be used to analyze large amounts of data to identify trends and patterns, helping FMCG companies make informed decisions about product development, pricing, and marketing.

4: Augmented Reality (AR) and Virtual Reality (VR): AR and VR technologies can be used to create immersive shopping experiences for consumers, allowing them to visualize products in their own space before making a purchase.

5: Robotics: Robotics can be used in warehouses and manufacturing facilities to automate repetitive tasks, increase efficiency, and reduce the risk of human error.

B: Potential Applications and Benefits

1: Supply Chain Management: Blockchain technology can improve transparency and traceability in the supply chain, reducing the risk of counterfeit products and improving overall efficiency.

2: Inventory Management: IoT devices can be used to track inventory levels in real-time, reducing the risk of stockouts and overstocking.

3: Personalized Marketing: AI can analyze customer data to create personalized marketing campaigns that are more likely to resonate with individual consumers.

4: Enhanced Customer Experience: AR and VR technologies can provide consumers with immersive shopping experiences, leading to increased engagement and satisfaction.

5: Cost Reduction: Robotics and automation can reduce labor costs and improve efficiency in manufacturing and warehouse operations.

6: Sustainability: Emerging technologies can help FMCG companies reduce their environmental impact by optimizing production processes and reducing waste.

By leveraging emerging technologies such as blockchain, IoT, AI, AR, VR, and robotics, FMCG companies can improve their operations, enhance customer experiences, and stay competitive in a rapidly evolving market.

Chapter 38: Inclusive Marketing

A: Strategies for Inclusive Marketing in FMCG

1: Diversity and Representation: Ensure that your marketing campaigns reflect the diversity of your target audience. Use inclusive imagery, language, and messaging that resonate with people of different backgrounds, cultures, and identities.

2: Accessibility: Make your products and marketing materials accessible to people with disabilities. This may include providing alternative formats, such as braille or audio, and ensuring that your website and digital content are accessible to screen readers.

3: Gender Neutrality: Avoid gender stereotypes in your marketing campaigns and product packaging. Use inclusive language and imagery that does not reinforce traditional gender roles.

4: Cultural Sensitivity: Be sensitive to cultural differences and avoid cultural appropriation in your marketing campaigns. Consult with cultural experts or community members to ensure that your messaging is respectful and inclusive.

5: Collaborations and Partnerships: Collaborate with influencers, organizations, or community groups that represent diverse audiences to reach new markets and build credibility with these communities.

B: Case Studies of Successful Inclusive Marketing Campaigns

1: Coca-Cola: Coca-Cola's "Share a Coke" campaign featured bottles with popular names from different cultures and backgrounds, encouraging people to share a Coke with friends and family members. The campaign was successful in promoting inclusivity and personalization.

2: Dove: Dove's "Real Beauty" campaign challenged traditional beauty standards by featuring women of all shapes, sizes, and skin tones in its advertising. The campaign was praised for its positive portrayal of diversity and inclusivity.

3: Procter & Gamble: Procter & Gamble's "The Talk" campaign addressed racial bias and inequality by depicting conversations that black parents have with their children about racism. The campaign was widely acclaimed for its powerful message of inclusivity and social justice.

4: Nike: Nike's "Dream Crazier" campaign featured female athletes breaking barriers and challenging stereotypes in sports. The campaign was celebrated for its empowering message of inclusivity and gender equality.

5: Airbnb: Airbnb's "We Accept" campaign promoted diversity and inclusion by highlighting its commitment to providing a welcoming and inclusive platform for travelers of all backgrounds. The campaign resonated with audiences and helped enhance Airbnb's brand reputation.

By implementing these strategies for inclusive marketing and learning from successful case studies, FMCG companies can create more inclusive and impactful marketing campaigns that resonate with diverse audiences and drive positive change.

Chapter 39: Employee Training and Development

A: Importance of Training and Development in FMCG Companies

1: Skill Enhancement: Training and development programs help employees acquire new skills and knowledge that are essential for their roles in FMCG companies. This includes training on new technologies, products, and industry trends.

2: Employee Engagement and Retention: Providing opportunities for training and development can increase employee engagement and job satisfaction, leading to higher retention rates. Employees are more likely to stay with a company that invests in their professional growth.

3: Improved Performance: Training and development programs can improve employee performance by enhancing their skills and knowledge. This can lead to increased productivity, efficiency, and quality of work.

4: Adaptability to Change: FMCG companies operate in a dynamic and competitive market where change is constant. Training and development programs help employees adapt to changes in technology, market trends, and consumer preferences.

5: Innovation and Creativity: Training and development can stimulate innovation and creativity among employees by exposing them to new ideas, perspectives, and ways of thinking.

6: Succession Planning: Training and development programs help identify and develop future leaders within the organization, ensuring a smooth transition in key roles and positions.

B: Strategies for Building a Skilled Workforce

1: Needs Assessment: Conduct a thorough needs assessment to identify the skills and knowledge gaps within the organization. This will help tailor training and development programs to meet specific needs.

2: Continuous Learning Culture: Foster a culture of continuous learning where employees are encouraged to seek out learning opportunities and develop their skills on an ongoing basis.

3: Mentorship and Coaching: Provide employees with access to mentors and coaches who can provide guidance, support, and feedback on their professional development.

4: Online Learning Platforms: Use online learning platforms to provide employees with access to a wide range of training courses and resources that they can use to develop their skills at their own pace.

5: Cross-Functional Training: Encourage employees to participate in cross-functional training programs that expose them to different areas of the business and help them develop a broader skill set.

6: Recognition and Rewards: Recognize and reward employees who actively participate in training and development programs and demonstrate a commitment to their professional growth.

By implementing these strategies, FMCG companies can build a skilled workforce that is capable of driving innovation, adapting to change, and achieving long-term success in a competitive market.

Chapter 40: Influencer Marketing

A: Role of Influencers in Promoting FMCG Products

1: Reach and Engagement: Influencers have a large and engaged following on social media platforms, making them effective at reaching and engaging with target audiences.

2: Authenticity and Trust: Influencers often have a strong relationship of trust with their followers, who view them as authentic and credible sources of information. This makes influencer marketing more effective than traditional advertising.

3: Product Recommendations: Influencers can promote FMCG products through sponsored posts, reviews, and endorsements, effectively showcasing the benefits and features of the products to their followers.

4: Brand Awareness: Collaborating with influencers can help FMCG companies increase brand awareness and reach new audiences who may not be familiar with their products.

5: Content Creation: Influencers are skilled at creating engaging and visually appealing content that showcases FMCG products in a compelling way, helping to generate interest and drive sales.

B: Best Practices for Working with Influencers

1: Set Clear Goals: Define clear objectives for your influencer marketing campaign, such as increasing brand awareness, driving sales, or promoting a new product launch.

2: Identify the Right Influencers: Choose influencers whose values, audience, and content align with your brand and target audience. Look for influencers with a high level of engagement and authenticity.

3: Establish Clear Expectations: Clearly communicate your expectations to influencers regarding the content, messaging, and deliverables of the campaign. Ensure that both parties are aligned on the scope of work and timeline.

4: Provide Creative Freedom: Allow influencers to be creative and authentic in their content creation, while ensuring that it aligns with your brand's guidelines and values.

5: Disclosure and Transparency: Ensure that influencers disclose any sponsored content in compliance with relevant regulations and guidelines. Transparency is key to maintaining trust with their audience.

6: Measure and Analyze Results: Use tracking tools and analytics to measure the effectiveness of your influencer marketing campaign. Evaluate key metrics such as reach, engagement, and conversion rates to determine the success of the campaign.

7: Build Long-Term Relationships: Consider building long-term relationships with influencers who have performed well in previous campaigns. This can lead to more authentic and impactful partnerships over time.

By following these best practices, FMCG companies can effectively leverage influencer marketing to promote their products, increase brand awareness, and engage with their target audience in a meaningful way.

Chapter 41: Risk Management

A: Identifying and Managing Risks in the FMCG Industry

1: Supply Chain Risks: FMCG companies are susceptible to supply chain disruptions, such as raw material shortages, transportation delays, and supplier failures. These risks can impact production, distribution, and product availability.

2: Market Risks: FMCG companies face market risks related to changing consumer preferences, competitive pressures, and economic conditions. These risks can affect sales, pricing, and market share.

3: Regulatory Risks: FMCG companies operate in a highly regulated environment, facing risks related to compliance with food safety, labeling, and advertising regulations. Non-compliance can result in fines, legal action, and damage to reputation.

4: Brand Risks: FMCG companies rely heavily on brand reputation and consumer trust. Risks such as product recalls, quality issues, or negative publicity can damage brand reputation and impact sales.

5: Operational Risks: FMCG companies face operational risks related to production, distribution, and logistics. These risks include equipment failures, workforce issues, and supply chain disruptions.

6: Financial Risks: FMCG companies are exposed to financial risks such as fluctuating commodity prices, currency exchange rates, and interest rates. These risks can impact profitability and financial performance.

B: Developing a Risk Management Framework

1: Identify Risks: Conduct a thorough risk assessment to identify and prioritize risks based on their potential impact and likelihood of occurrence. Consider both internal and external factors that could affect the business.

2: Assess and Evaluate Risks: Evaluate the potential impact of identified risks on the business, taking into account factors such as financial impact, operational disruption, and reputational damage. Assess the likelihood of each risk occurring.

3: Develop Risk Mitigation Strategies: Develop strategies to mitigate or manage identified risks. This may include implementing controls, diversifying suppliers, securing insurance coverage, or developing contingency plans.

4: Monitor and Review: Regularly monitor and review the effectiveness of risk mitigation strategies. Update the risk management framework as needed based on changes in the business environment or new emerging risks.

5: Communication and Reporting: Ensure that risk management processes are well-communicated and understood across the organization. Report on risk management activities to senior management and stakeholders regularly.

6: Continuous Improvement: Continuously review and improve the risk management framework to address new and emerging risks. Incorporate lessons learned from past experiences to strengthen risk management practices.

By developing and implementing a robust risk management framework, FMCG companies can identify, assess, and mitigate risks effectively, ensuring business resilience and continuity in a volatile and competitive market environment.

Chapter 42: Product Innovation Process

A: Steps Involved in Developing and Launching New FMCG Products

1: Idea Generation: The first step in the product innovation process is to generate ideas for new products. This can be done through brainstorming sessions, market research, and consumer feedback.

2: Concept Development: Once ideas are generated, they are developed into concepts. Concepts outline the basic idea of the product, including its features, benefits, and target market.

3: Feasibility Analysis: A feasibility analysis is conducted to determine the technical, financial, and market feasibility of the product concept. This involves assessing factors such as production costs, market demand, and competition.

4: Product Development: If the concept is deemed feasible, the product development process begins. This involves designing the product, developing prototypes, and conducting tests to ensure that the product meets quality and performance standards.

5: Market Testing: Before launching the product, it is tested in the market to gather feedback from consumers. This helps identify any potential issues and allows for adjustments to be made before full-scale production.

6: Commercialization: Once the product has been tested and refined, it is ready for commercialization. This involves finalizing the marketing strategy, setting pricing, and launching the product in the market.

7: Post-Launch Evaluation: After the product is launched, it is important to evaluate its performance and gather feedback from consumers. This helps identify areas for improvement and informs future product development efforts.

B: Best Practices for Fostering Innovation

1: Encourage Creativity: Create a work environment that encourages employees to think creatively and come up with new ideas. This can be done through brainstorming sessions, innovation challenges, and rewards for innovative ideas.

2: Cross-Functional Collaboration: Foster collaboration between different departments, such as marketing, R&D, and operations, to leverage diverse perspectives and expertise in the innovation process.

3: Customer-Centric Approach: Focus on understanding customer needs and preferences to develop products that truly address their pain points and deliver value.

4: Agile Development: Adopt agile development methodologies to quickly iterate on product ideas and respond to changing market conditions.

5: Continuous Learning: Encourage employees to continuously learn and stay updated on industry trends, technologies, and best practices in product innovation.

6: Risk-Taking Culture: Create a culture that encourages risk-taking and experimentation, as innovation often involves taking calculated risks.

7: Reward Innovation: Recognize and reward employees for their innovative ideas and contributions to the product development process.

By following these best practices, FMCG companies can foster a culture of innovation and develop new products that meet the evolving needs of consumers and drive business growth.

Chapter 43: Customer Relationship Management (CRM)

A: Importance of CRM in FMCG

1: Customer Retention: CRM helps FMCG companies retain existing customers by providing personalized experiences and addressing their specific needs and preferences.

2: Customer Loyalty: By building strong relationships with customers, CRM helps FMCG companies foster loyalty and increase customer lifetime value.

3: Targeted Marketing: CRM enables FMCG companies to segment their customer base and target specific customer groups with personalized marketing messages, leading to higher conversion rates.

4: Improved Customer Service: CRM allows FMCG companies to track customer interactions and provide timely and personalized customer service, leading to higher levels of satisfaction.

5: Data-driven Decision Making: CRM provides valuable insights into customer behavior, preferences, and trends, enabling FMCG companies to make informed decisions and drive business growth.

6: Competitive Advantage: A well-implemented CRM strategy can provide FMCG companies with a competitive advantage by helping them better understand and serve their customers compared to competitors.

B: Strategies for Building and Maintaining Customer Relationships

1: Personalization: Use CRM data to personalize interactions with customers, such as personalized marketing messages, product recommendations, and offers based on their purchase history and preferences.

2: Customer Segmentation: Segment your customer base into groups based on demographics, behavior, and preferences, and tailor your marketing strategies and communications to each segment.

3: Communication Channels: Use multiple communication channels, such as email, social media, and mobile apps, to engage with customers and provide them with relevant and timely information.

4: Feedback and Surveys: Regularly seek feedback from customers through surveys and feedback forms to understand their needs and preferences better.

5: Customer Service Excellence: Provide exceptional customer service by responding promptly to customer inquiries, resolving issues quickly, and going above and beyond to meet customer needs.

6: Loyalty Programs: Implement loyalty programs to reward customers for their repeat purchases and encourage them to continue buying from your brand.

7: Continuous Improvement: Continuously review and refine your CRM strategies based on customer feedback and market trends to ensure that they remain effective in building and maintaining customer relationships.

By implementing these strategies, FMCG companies can effectively use CRM to build strong and lasting relationships with their customers, leading to increased loyalty, higher retention rates, and sustainable business growth.

Chapter 44: Global Sourcing and Procurement

A: Strategies for Sourcing Raw Materials and Components Globally

1: Supplier Diversity: Develop relationships with a diverse range of suppliers to reduce dependency on any single supplier and mitigate risks associated with supply chain disruptions.

2: Cost Optimization: Identify cost-effective sourcing options by comparing prices, negotiating contracts, and leveraging economies of scale.

3: Quality Assurance: Implement stringent quality control measures to ensure that sourced raw materials and components meet the required quality standards.

4: Just-in-Time Inventory: Adopt a just-in-time inventory management approach to minimize inventory holding costs and improve efficiency in the supply chain.

5: Strategic Partnerships: Establish strategic partnerships with key suppliers to secure preferential pricing, access to new technologies, and priority in supply allocation.

6: Local Sourcing: Consider sourcing raw materials and components locally to reduce lead times, transportation costs, and dependency on international suppliers.

B: Managing Risks in Global Supply Chains

1: Supply Chain Visibility: Enhance visibility into your supply chain by leveraging technologies such as blockchain and IoT to track and trace products throughout the supply chain.

2: Risk Assessment: Conduct regular risk assessments to identify potential risks in your global supply chain, such as geopolitical risks, natural disasters, and supplier financial instability.

3: Diversification: Diversify your supplier base and sourcing locations to reduce risks associated with disruptions in any single region or supplier.

4: Contingency Planning: Develop contingency plans to address potential supply chain disruptions, such as alternative sourcing options, safety stock, and emergency response protocols.

5: Collaboration: Collaborate with suppliers, industry partners, and government agencies to share information and best practices for managing risks in the global supply chain.

6: Continuous Improvement: Continuously monitor and improve your global sourcing and procurement processes to enhance efficiency, reduce costs, and mitigate risks in the supply chain.

By implementing these strategies, FMCG companies can effectively source raw materials and components globally while managing risks in their supply chains, ensuring a reliable and efficient supply of products to meet customer demand.

Chapter 45: Green Marketing

A: Strategies for Promoting Environmentally Friendly Products

1: Product Innovation: Develop environmentally friendly products that are made from sustainable materials, use less energy, or produce less waste. Highlight these features in your marketing materials to appeal to environmentally conscious consumers.

2: Eco-Friendly Packaging: Use recyclable or biodegradable packaging for your products and promote this in your marketing campaigns. Consider reducing packaging waste by using minimalist packaging designs.

3: Energy Efficiency: Emphasize the energy efficiency of your products, such as appliances or electronics, to appeal to consumers looking to reduce their energy consumption and carbon footprint.

4: Carbon Footprint Reduction: Communicate efforts to reduce your company's carbon footprint, such as using renewable energy sources or implementing energy-saving practices in your operations.

5: Corporate Social Responsibility (CSR): Highlight your company's commitment to environmental sustainability through CSR initiatives, such as tree planting campaigns or beach cleanups, and integrate these into your marketing efforts.

6: Educate Consumers: Educate consumers about the environmental impact of their purchasing decisions and how choosing your environmentally friendly products can contribute to a more sustainable future.

B: Green Certifications and Their Impact on Consumer Perception

1: Organic Certification: Products certified as organic are perceived to be free from synthetic chemicals and pesticides, appealing to consumers looking for natural and environmentally friendly options.

2: Energy Star Certification: Products with Energy Star certification are recognized for their energy efficiency, leading to cost savings for consumers and reducing their environmental impact.

3: Fair Trade Certification: Fair Trade certified products are produced using environmentally sustainable practices and ensure fair wages and working conditions for producers, appealing to consumers concerned about social and environmental issues.

4: Eco-Labeling: Eco-labels, such as the Forest Stewardship Council (FSC) label for sustainable forestry practices, provide assurance to consumers that products are sourced or produced in an environmentally responsible manner.

5: Green Seal Certification: Products with Green Seal certification meet rigorous environmental standards, giving consumers confidence that they are making a sustainable choice.

6: Consumer Perception: Green certifications can enhance consumer perception of a brand's commitment to sustainability and influence purchasing decisions, particularly among environmentally conscious consumers.

By incorporating these strategies and certifications into your green marketing efforts, you can effectively promote environmentally friendly products and appeal to consumers seeking sustainable options, ultimately driving sales and building a positive brand image.

Chapter 46: Product Placement and Merchandising

A: Importance of Product Placement in FMCG Retail

1: Visibility: Strategic product placement ensures that FMCG products are prominently displayed and easily accessible to customers, increasing the likelihood of purchase.

2: Brand Awareness: Effective product placement helps increase brand awareness by showcasing products in high-traffic areas where they are more likely to be noticed by consumers.

3: Impulse Purchases: Placing products in strategic locations, such as near checkout counters or at eye level, can encourage impulse purchases, driving sales.

4: Cross-Selling and Upselling: Product placement can be used to promote complementary products or upsell customers to premium products, increasing the average transaction value.

5: Seasonal and Promotional Displays: Product placement can be used to highlight seasonal promotions or new product launches, driving excitement and boosting sales.

B: Merchandising Techniques to Drive Sales

1: Eye-Level Placement: Place products at eye level to increase visibility and ensure that they are easily noticed by customers.

2: Cross-Merchandising: Group complementary products together to encourage cross-selling. For example, display chips next to salsa or crackers next to cheese.

3: Endcap Displays: Use endcap displays at the end of aisles to showcase featured products or promotions, attracting the attention of customers as they walk by.

4: Point-of-Purchase (POP) Displays: Use POP displays near checkout counters to promote impulse purchases, such as small snacks or beverages.

5: Seasonal and Theme-Based Displays: Create seasonal or theme-based displays to attract customers' attention and drive sales. For example, create a back-to-school display featuring lunchbox essentials.

6: Interactive Displays: Use interactive displays, such as touchscreens or virtual reality experiences, to engage customers and promote products in a unique way.

7: Signage and Visual Merchandising: Use signage and visual merchandising techniques, such as color blocking or product grouping, to create visually appealing displays that draw customers in.

8: Product Sampling: Offer product samples to customers to encourage trial and purchase. Sampling can be particularly effective for new or unfamiliar products.

By implementing these merchandising techniques, FMCG retailers can optimize product placement and drive sales, ultimately enhancing the overall shopping experience for customers.

Chapter 47: Data Privacy and Security

A: Importance of Data Privacy in FMCG

1: Consumer Trust: Protecting consumer data is essential for maintaining trust. Consumers are more likely to engage with brands that respect their privacy and safeguard their personal information.

2: Legal Compliance: FMCG companies are required to comply with data protection laws and regulations, such as the General Data Protection Regulation (GDPR) in Europe and the California Consumer Privacy Act (CCPA) in the United States. Failure to comply can result in hefty fines and damage to reputation.

3: Brand Reputation: Data breaches or mishandling of customer data can damage brand reputation and erode consumer trust. It can take years to rebuild trust once it has been lost.

4: Competitive Advantage: Prioritizing data privacy can be a competitive advantage, as consumers are increasingly aware of privacy issues and are more likely to choose companies that take data protection seriously.

5: Consumer Expectations: Consumers expect their data to be handled responsibly and securely. Meeting these expectations can help build stronger relationships with customers.

B: Strategies for Ensuring Data Security

1: Data Encryption: Encrypt sensitive data both in transit and at rest to protect it from unauthorized access.

2: Access Control: Implement strict access controls to ensure that only authorized personnel have access to sensitive data.

3: Regular Audits and Assessments: Conduct regular security audits and assessments to identify and address vulnerabilities in your data security practices.

4: Employee Training: Provide regular training to employees on data privacy best practices and how to recognize and respond to potential security threats.

5: Secure Data Storage: Use secure methods for storing data, such as cloud-based storage with encryption and multi-factor authentication.

6: Data Minimization: Collect only the data that is necessary for your business operations and ensure that it is stored securely.

7: Incident Response Plan: Develop and implement an incident response plan to quickly respond to and mitigate the effects of data breaches or security incidents.

8: Privacy by Design: Incorporate data privacy and security considerations into the design of your products and services from the outset.

By implementing these strategies, FMCG companies can protect consumer data, comply with regulations, and build trust with their customers, ultimately enhancing their brand reputation and competitive position.

Chapter 48: Legal and Regulatory Compliance

A: Regulatory Requirements for FMCG Companies

1: Product Labeling: FMCG companies must comply with regulations regarding product labeling, including providing accurate and clear information about ingredients, nutritional content, and allergens.

2: Advertising and Marketing: Regulations govern advertising and marketing practices for FMCG companies, including restrictions on false or misleading claims and advertising to children.

3: Food Safety: FMCG companies in the food and beverage industry must comply with food safety regulations to ensure that products are safe for consumption.

4: Packaging and Waste Management: Regulations may require FMCG companies to adhere to certain packaging and waste management standards to reduce environmental impact.

5: Labor Laws: FMCG companies must comply with labor laws and regulations related to employment practices, including working conditions, wages, and hours of work.

6: Environmental Regulations: FMCG companies must comply with environmental regulations related to waste disposal, emissions, and sustainability practices.

B: Strategies for Ensuring Compliance

1: Stay Informed: Keep abreast of changes in regulations that affect the FMCG industry by regularly monitoring regulatory updates and industry news.

2: Conduct Audits: Conduct regular audits of your operations to ensure compliance with relevant regulations and identify areas for improvement.

3: Employee Training: Provide training to employees on relevant regulations and best practices for compliance.

4: Legal Counsel: Consult with legal counsel to ensure that your business practices comply with applicable laws and regulations.

5: Documentation and Record Keeping: Maintain accurate and up-to-date records of your compliance efforts, including policies, procedures, and training records.

6: Collaboration with Regulatory Bodies: Work closely with regulatory bodies and industry associations to stay informed about regulatory changes and ensure compliance.

7: Continuous Improvement: Continuously review and improve your compliance processes to adapt to changing regulatory requirements and mitigate compliance risks.

By implementing these strategies, FMCG companies can ensure compliance with relevant regulations, reduce regulatory risks, and maintain a positive reputation with consumers and regulatory bodies.

Chapter 49: Market Research and Consumer Insights

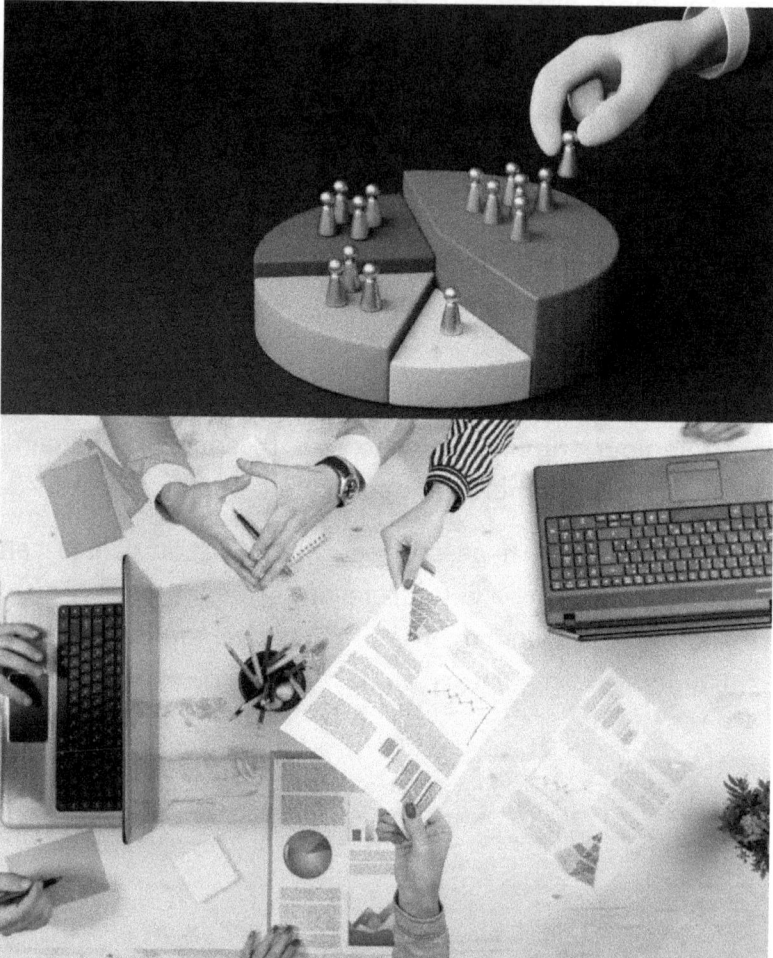

A: Importance of Market Research in FMCG

1: Understanding Consumer Needs: Market research helps FMCG companies understand consumer preferences, behaviors, and needs, enabling them to develop products and marketing strategies that resonate with their target audience.

2: Identifying Market Trends: Market research allows FMCG companies to stay abreast of market trends, such as changing consumer preferences, emerging technologies, and competitive landscape, helping them make informed business decisions.

3: New Product Development: Market research provides insights into market gaps and opportunities, guiding FMCG companies in developing new products that meet consumer needs and preferences.

4: Pricing and Promotion Strategies: Market research helps FMCG companies determine optimal pricing strategies and promotional tactics to attract and retain customers.

5: Brand Perception: Market research helps FMCG companies understand how their brand is perceived in the market, allowing them to make strategic decisions to enhance brand image and loyalty.

6: Competitive Analysis: Market research enables FMCG companies to analyze competitors' strategies, strengths, and weaknesses, helping them differentiate their products and gain a competitive edge.

B: Techniques for Gathering and Analyzing Consumer Insights

1: Surveys and Questionnaires: Conduct surveys and questionnaires to gather quantitative data on consumer preferences, purchasing behavior, and brand perception.

2: Focus Groups: Organize focus groups to gather qualitative insights from a small group of consumers, allowing for in-depth discussions and exploration of topics.

3: Interviews: Conduct one-on-one interviews with consumers to gain deeper insights into their preferences, motivations, and behaviors.

4: Observational Research: Observe consumers in their natural environment to understand their behavior, preferences, and decision-making processes.

5: Social Media Listening: Monitor social media channels to gather insights into consumer sentiment, trends, and feedback about your products and brand.

6: Data Analytics: Use data analytics tools to analyze large datasets and extract meaningful insights into consumer behavior, trends, and patterns.

7: Ethnographic Research: Conduct ethnographic research to study consumer behavior and culture in real-life settings, providing deep insights into consumer lifestyles and habits.

8: Online Reviews and Feedback: Monitor online reviews and feedback about your products to understand consumer perceptions and identify areas for improvement.

By utilizing these techniques, FMCG companies can gather valuable consumer insights that inform their marketing, product development, and business strategies, ultimately driving growth and success in the market.

Chapter 50: Conclusion and Future Outlook

A: Key Takeaways from the Book

1: Importance of Innovation: Innovation is crucial for FMCG companies to stay competitive and meet evolving consumer needs. Product innovation, packaging innovation, and sustainability initiatives are key areas of focus.

2: Customer-Centric Approach: FMCG companies need to adopt a customer-centric approach, focusing on understanding consumer preferences, building strong relationships, and delivering personalized experiences.

3: Data-Driven Decision Making: Data analytics plays a critical role in FMCG companies' decision-making processes, helping them understand market trends, consumer behavior, and optimize their operations.

4: Regulatory Compliance: FMCG companies must comply with a complex set of regulations related to product labeling, advertising, food safety, and environmental sustainability to avoid legal issues and maintain consumer trust.

5: Market Research and Consumer Insights: Continuous market research and gathering consumer insights are essential for FMCG companies to stay ahead of trends, innovate effectively, and meet consumer expectations.

B: Predictions for the Future of the FMCG Industry

1: Continued Growth in E-commerce: The FMCG industry will see continued growth in e-commerce sales, driven by changing consumer shopping habits and the convenience of online shopping.

2: Focus on Sustainability: Sustainability will become a key focus for FMCG companies, with consumers increasingly demanding environmentally friendly products and packaging.

3: Personalized Marketing: FMCG companies will increasingly use data analytics and AI to personalize marketing messages and offers, enhancing the customer experience.

4: Rise of DTC Brands: Direct-to-consumer (DTC) brands will continue to gain popularity, offering unique products and cutting out traditional retail channels.

5: Health and Wellness Trends: FMCG companies will see increased demand for health-focused products, including organic, natural, and functional foods and beverages.

6: Continued Innovation: FMCG companies will need to continue innovating in products, packaging, and marketing strategies to stay competitive in a rapidly evolving market.

In conclusion, the FMCG industry is poised for continued growth and innovation, driven by changing consumer preferences, technological advancements, and a focus on sustainability and health. Companies that adapt to these trends and embrace innovation will thrive in the future.

www.ingramcontent.com/pod-product-compliance
Lightning Source LLC
Chambersburg PA
CBHW052204220526
45471CB00004B/1810